Collins
INTERNATIONAL
PRIMARY

Computing
Teacher's Guide

1

Rebecca Franks, Dr Tracy Gardner and Liz Smart

William Collins' dream of knowledge for all began with the publication of his first book in 1819.

A self-educated mill worker, he not only enriched millions of lives, but also founded a flourishing publishing house. Today, staying true to this spirit, Collins books are packed with inspiration, innovation and practical expertise. They place you at the centre of a world of possibility and give you exactly what you need to explore it.

Collins. Freedom to teach

Published by Collins

An imprint of HarperCollinsPublishers
The News Building, 1 London Bridge Street,
London,
SE1 9GF, UK

HarperCollinsPublishers
Macken House, 39/40 Mayor Street Upper, Dublin 1,
D01 C9W8, Ireland

Browse the complete Collins catalogue at collins.co.uk

10 9 8 7 6 5 4 3 2 1

ISBN 978-0-00-868396-2

British Library Cataloguing-in-Publication Data
A catalogue record for this publication is available from the British Library.

Authors: Rebecca Franks, Dr Tracy Gardner and Liz Smart
Publisher: Catherine Martin
Product manager: Saaleh Patel
Project manager: Just Content Ltd
Development editor: Gemma Coleman
Copyeditor: Tanya Solomons
Proofreader: Laura Connell
Cover designer: Gordon McGilp
Cover illustrator: Amparo Barrera, Kneath Associates
Internal designer: Sam Vail
Illustration: Jouve Ltd
Typesetter: Sam Vail
Production controller: Lyndsey Rogers
Printed and bound by Ashford Colour Press

MIX
Paper | Supporting responsible forestry
FSC
www.fsc.org FSC™ C007454

This book contains FSC™ certified paper and other controlled sources to ensure responsible forest management.

For more information visit: www.harpercollins.co.uk/green

Acknowledgements

Support materials and screenshots are licensed under the Creative Commons Attribution-ShareAlike 2.0 license. We are grateful to the following for permission to reproduce screenshots. In some instances, we have been unable to trace the owners of copyright material, and we would appreciate any information that would enable us to do so.

Scratch Foundation: Authorised usage of screenshots showcasing Scratch programming environment elements.

Scratch is developed by the Lifelong Kindergarten Group at the MIT Media Lab: p.11, p.17–20, p.34–48, p.51, p.68, p.71, p.81–82.

Contents

Teacher's Guide

Introduction

Stage 1 Computing provides a comprehensive foundation in computing and digital literacy. It serves as an introductory step for learners who may not have essential digital skills, such as typing and navigating a screen using a mouse. Throughout this stage, learners will explore a wide range of skills related to the everyday technologies around them.

Overview

The Collins series is built around six themes relating to computing and digital literacy.

- Our digital world - Providing the tools and insights into safely navigating the digital world around us
- Content creation - Creating content effectively using a variety of software, from office tools to video production
- Create with code – Learning the fundamentals of programming and computational thinking skills
- How computers work – Discovering the specific technologies that make up a computer system
- Connect the world – Exploring how the world is connected through networks, the internet and the World Wide Web
- The power of data - Collecting, analysing and presenting data linked to real-world activities that create or empower change

Stage 1 has seven chapters that relate directly to these six themes, with two chapters dedicated to creating with code.

Stage 1 Kit list

Chapter 1 – Our digital world	<ul><li>Examples of computers in your local environment</li><li>A 'special guest' from the school community to interview</li><li>Coloured pencils or crayons</li></ul>
Chapter 2 – Content creation	<ul><li>Access to computers</li><li>Usernames and passwords for your computers / learners</li><li>Word processing software</li><li>Scratch 3 – either the desktop app or online accounts</li></ul>
Chapter 3 – Create with code 1	<ul><li>Copies of your class register</li><li>Bee-Bots or equivalent (enough for one for each small group)</li><li>Objects or printed photographs to create a story</li><li>A piece of paper (starting mat for Bee-Bot)</li></ul>
Chapter 4 – How computers work	<ul><li>Access to computers that can play and record sound</li><li>Scratch 3 – either the desktop app or online accounts</li></ul>

Chapter 5 – Create with code 2	• A stacking ring toy or paper-based version • Access to computers • Scratch 3 – either the desktop app or online accounts • Glue • Scissors • Coloured pencils • Chapter 5.3 worksheet for each learner/pair
Chapter 6 – Connect the world	• Cups and string • Plain paper
Chapter 7 – The power of data	• Access to computers • Spreadsheet software • Form-generation software

Pedagogy

Our overall approach

Our approach to teaching is based on the latest research in ensuring that computing classrooms are inclusive environments that foster greater participation of underestimated groups in computing and technology.

Each chapter is carefully organised to develop essential knowledge and skills whilst working towards the creation of a final project. The final projects are designed to boost creative skills and give learners the opportunity to make decisions and develop artefacts that matter to them. All chapters end with a showcase lesson that gives learners the opportunity to develop their presenting skills, whilst gaining valuable feedback on their work.

Every lesson plan states the key pedagogy that is used in that lesson. Stage 1 uses the following key pedagogies.

Classroom talk

Classroom talk is the communication that happens in a classroom, between teacher and learner, learner and teacher, and between learners. Discussion and social interaction plays an important role in computing education. Throughout every lesson in Stage 1 you will find 'Discuss' activities. You are encouraged to incorporate topics that have been generated by learners and encourage them to share their ideas and perspectives and to ask any questions they have.

Benefits:
- Classroom talk provides an opportunity for multi-way knowledge sharing and building a shared understanding.
- Valuing student voices and perspectives increases their sense of connection to computing.

Read more about the research:
Jenkins, 2017. Classroom Talk and Computational Thinking DOI: (<u>Website IntR1</u>)

Design-thinking

Design-thinking is an approach to building projects that focuses on the needs of the user. It is an iterative process that has five parts: Empathise, Define, Ideate, Prototype and Test. In Stage 1 learners participate in a simplified design-thinking process in the project for every chapter. Learners build design-thinking skills by empathising with a person who could be helped by a robot and making a prototype of a web page.

Benefits:
- Develops empathy and an understanding of human-computer interaction.
- An approach used in industry to create innovative products, meaning learners are developing valuable skills for life.
- Connects learners to the value of projects that can be created with computing.

Read more about the research:
Rusmann et al, 2021. When design thinking goes to school: A literature review of design competences for the K-12 level. DOI: (<u>Website IntR2</u>)

Get creative

This key pedagogy is used to encourage learners to be creative with code or technology and provides them with the freedom to make their own design choices. Stage 1 provides a wealth of opportunities to get creative with technology from designing their own robots to creating an animated window scene.

Benefits:
- Learners create projects that are culturally relevant to them, leading to greater engagement.
- Providing more choice in the project that learners create leads to a greater sense of agency, particularly amongst girls.
- Spending more time on the creative elements of computing leads to greater engagement of underestimated groups.

Human et al, 2022. Gender balance in Computing - Evaluation of the Relevance Intervention. (<u>Website IntR3</u>)

Parsons problems

A Parsons Problem is an activity in which learners are given all of the blocks or lines of code needed to solve a problem, but not in the right order. Learners have to rearrange the code into the correct order.

Benefits:
- Learners focus on complete units of code (lines or blocks) rather than the elements they are made from, building higher-level understanding.
- Learners can focus on only the important aspects of a problem, reducing cognitive load.
- Learners do not have to enter large amounts of code so they can complete problems more quickly.

Read more about the research:
Du et al, 2020. A Review of Research on Parsons Problems DOI: (<u>Website IntR4</u>)

Showcase

Showcasing is presenting a project to an audience. In Stage 1, every chapter ends with a showcase of the work that learners have completed.

There are lots of ways that you can carry out a showcase in your setting. You can choose an option most suited to your class. For example:

- Each learner presents their project to the whole class.
- Divide the class into small groups. Each learner presents their project to their group.
- Split the class in half. Half of the class present whilst the other half act as the audience. Swap roles.

Benefits:
- Showcasing requires learners to reflect on their work so that they can explain it to others.
- Showcasing develops important communication skills.
- Showcasing enables learners in the audience to develop the ability to give feedback.
- Showcasing provides an opportunity to celebrate the achievements of learners and the tangible outcomes of computing work.

Develop practical skills

To be effective in computing, learners need to develop practical skills such as using a keyboard and mouse and using IT tools.

Benefits:
- Developing practical skills enables learners to become effective users of technology.
- Developing practical skills means that learners have more capacity to focus on the new computing concepts they are learning.

Role play

Role play activities involve learners acting out scenarios to reinforce concepts that they are learning. In Stage 1, learners role play taking the class register as an example of an algorithm and asking and telling a grown-up when staying safe when using computers.
Benefits:
- Role play activities allow learners to gain practical experience of an activity.
- Role play is engaging for learners and helps them to remember important ideas.

Roleplay is a well-established practice in teaching. It has not been extensively studied in computing education for children.

Unplugged

Unplugged activities demonstrate computing concepts without using computers. Our unplugged activities are designed to relate directly to the technical concepts that learners are exploring. They follow a semantic wave (unplug, unpack, repack) while keeping closer to the technical concepts than other approaches to avoid confusion, particularly with respect to the international context. This means there is less need for 'unpack' and 'repack'. In Stage 1, wired connections and computer networks are introduced through unplugged activities.

Benefits:

- Unplugged activities have been demonstrated to positively affect learners computational thinking skills.
- Unplugged activities can increase learners' engagement with concepts and develop deeper understanding.
- Unplugged activities can be helpful when learners have limited access to computers.

Read more about the research:
Chen et al, 2023. Fostering computational thinking through unplugged activities: A systematic literature review and meta-analysis DOI: (Website IntR5)

Physical computing

Physical computing involves using tangible objects that children can interact with. In later stages, this can involve using motors and sensors. In Stage 1, learners use Bee-Bots, which are physical floor robots that they can touch and observe. They also learn about robots and computer input and output components such as a mouse and keyboard.

Benefits:

- Physical computing provides learners with additional context for understanding the results of their instructions or code.
- Physical computing is engaging and generates excitement and interest in the classroom.
- Physical computing provides a connection from computing to the physical devices that learners encounter in everyday life such as games consoles or supermarket checkout machines.

Read more about the research:
Hodges et al, 2020. Physical Computing: A Key Element of Modern Computer Science Education Computer. DOI: (Website IntR6)

Real-world contexts

Lessons make regular links to everyday life scenarios where learners may encounter the concepts they are learning about. Links are also made to other curriculum topics. In Stage 1, learners design a robot to help someone in their school and they plan a class party using data.
Benefits:

- Using real-world contexts aids learners' understanding by connecting computing concepts to their everyday lives.
- Real-world contexts demonstrate the value of computing, which engages a more diverse group of learners.
- Real-world contexts show the practical application of computing and make links to the world of work.

Working collaboratively

Working collaboratively means completing tasks in pairs or small groups. It includes group or pair programming. In Stage 1, learners complete many activities collaboratively including programming a floor robot. You can also put learners into pairs or small groups to work collaboratively on other activities. Lessons often encourage learners to review each other's work.

Benefits:
- Collaborative working can reduce cognitive load.
- Learners can complete work more quickly by working collaboratively.
- Collaborative working can lead to higher levels of engagement.
- Collaborative working reduces the number of physical resources, such as floor robots, needed for a class.

Read more about the research:
Lewis, 2010. Is pair programming more effective than other forms of collaboration for young students? DOI: (Website IntR7)

Assessment

The books are designed to follow a mastery learning approach where all learners are supported and challenged to meet the age related expectations of the curriculum. Formative assessment should be used regularly to check the overall understanding of your class. Each chapter has a final project that is assessed summatively. Appropriate scaffolding is provided to allow for the majority of learners to meet expectations.

Formative assessment in the student workbook

The student workbook provides opportunities for learners to apply their learning to various activities. The outcome of these tasks can be used as part of a formative assessment process to measure the learner progress throughout the chapter. Where a workbook question has a specific answer, answers have been provided. There are also 'model answers' to guide your assessment needs.

Formative assessment and the lesson plan guidance

Each lesson plan has a guidance column. Where appropriate, additional support has been provided for the type of answers that you are looking for when questioning the learning. This will help to guide your formative assessment. If learners are struggling to understand the concept then you should revisit it with the support of the scaffolding and guidance provided.

Summative assessment and the project rubrics

Every chapter has a final project that the learners are working towards. Each project has a project brief with requirements for learners to meet. The projects are then summatively assessed using a rubric. Each rubric has three columns 'Working towards', 'Meets expected', and 'Exceeding expected'. The majority of the class should be able to achieve the 'Meets expected' criteria. Some learners will exceed this expectation and go a step further than required by the project brief. A few learners may fall into the 'Working towards' category and should receive additional support and scaffolding.

Learners should have access to the rubric at the start of a project so that it is clear how they will be assessed. This also helps to support their metacognitive skills.

Summative assessment and showcasing

Each chapter ends with a showcase which provides an opportunity for summative assessment. Teachers can complete the assessment rubric during showcase lessons. Teachers can ask additional questions of learners to establish their understanding of specific criteria.

Hardware and software guidance

Scratch

Scratch is a free graphical block-based programming language developed for young people. It can be used to make animations, music, games, and more. The projects in Stage 1 use Scratch version 3.

Scratch 3 can be used online through a web browser on a laptop, desktop computer, or tablet. Alternatively, Scratch 3 can be used without internet connection by downloading and installing the offline version on a laptop or desktop computer. It is important to decide which option is best for you and practise using that method before a lesson with learners.

The online version of Scratch can be used with Scratch accounts. This enables learners to save their projects and open them in the future. Projects will save to their 'My Stuff' page. When using the online version of Scratch without accounts, learners will need to save their projects to the computer and load their projects from the computer.

Projects saved to Scratch accounts can remain 'private' to that learner, or be shared and viewed by others in the Scratch community. This option is chosen on a project- by-project basis.

With the online version of Scratch, you can set up a Teacher account. This is an alternative to a standard Scratch account and is used to create, manage and monitor learner accounts. A teacher account must be requested through the Educator section on the Scratch website. This should be done in advance of using Scratch in lessons for the first time as some preparation of student accounts will be required.

Some learner activities use a Scratch starter project. The starter projects are referenced in the 'You will need' in the Teacher's Guide. To use the starter projects online with accounts, you can give learners the project link and ask them to click 'remix' to save a copy to their account. If they are using the online version without accounts, they should use the link to open and then save a copy to their computer. If you are using Scratch offline, you will need to save the starter projects somewhere the learners can access and then ask them to save their copy to the computer.

Scratch can be accessed via (Website IntR8).

The following pages can be printed to give to learners. They detail the steps to open starter projects, save a copy, and reopen their copy in future.

Scratch online – use a starter project with a Scratch

Start your project

- Open the link your teacher has given you
- Click 'See inside'
  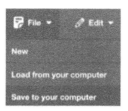
- Click 'File'
- Click 'Save to your computer'
  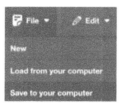
- Do the activity
- Save your project regularly

Open your project in the future

- Go to the Scratch website
- Click 'Create'
- Click 'File'
- Click 'Load from your computer'
- Find your file and click 'Open'
- Do the activity
- Save your project often

Scratch offline

Start your project

- Open the Scratch app

- Click 'File'

- Click 'Load from your computer'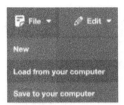

- Find the project your teacher has saved and click 'Open'
- Give your project a name

- Click 'File'

- Click 'Save to your computer'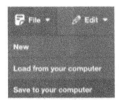

- Do the activity
- Save your project regularly

Open your project in the future

- Open the Scratch app

- Click 'File'

- Click 'Load from your computer'

- Find your file and click 'Open'
- Do the activity
- Save your project regularly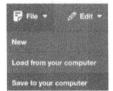

A microphone

There are activities that use Scratch to record sound. For these activities, a microphone will be required. The microphone can either be inbuilt into the computer or connected as an external device.

When using a microphone with Scratch for the first time on a device, Scratch will need permission to use the microphone. Click 'Allow' on the pop-up window.

If a learner accidentally blocks the microphone, you can access the settings for the page and 'allow' the microphone.

A visualiser (optional)

A visualiser is a camera that can be connected to a computer and used to project an image and zoom in. It is a useful piece of equipment to have available when showing physical resources to learners.

Bee-Bots

A Bee-Bot is a floor robot made by TTS.

Learners enter code using directional arrow buttons. The code is stored in the Bee-Bot memory and is run using the 'Go' button. There are additional buttons to pause the code and reset the memory.

The forward and backward buttons move the Bee-Bot 15cm in that direction each time the button press is read. The left and right buttons rotate the Bee-Bot 90 degrees (1 quarter turn) on the spot.

On the underside of the Bee-Bot is the charging socket and an on/off switch. There is also a sound button to mute and unmute the Bee-Bot.

There are different versions of the Bee-Bot but all work in a very similar way. There is a selection of grid-based mats available to purchase with your Bee-Bot but these are not required.

These books specifically mention the Bee-Bot, but there are alternatives on the market such as 'Code & Go Robot Mouse' by 'Learning Resources'. You can use this, and other floor robots, as an alternative, but note the slight differences (such as distance moved).

Online form software

Learners are required to use an online form that contains questions they have developed as a class. The Teacher's Guide references Google Forms as it is a free, web-based survey application that integrates nicely with the free web-based spreadsheet software Google Sheets. After creating a form, go to 'Responses' and click 'Link to Sheets' to set this up.

Google Forms can be accessed via (Website IntR9)

Alternative applications for online forms are available. If you use an online form application that doesn't link directly to spreadsheet software, you will need to manually input learner responses into a spreadsheet.

Word processing software

Learners will use a word processor to practise their typing skills. You may already have word processing software installed on your school computers. The Teacher's Guide references Google Docs, a free web-based application.

Google Docs can be accessed via (Website IntR10)

Keyboards

The activities can all be completed using external, built-in or digital keyboards. There is guidance next to activities in the Teacher's Guide where a slightly different combination of keys might be needed depending on your setup.

One example of this is using Caps Lock on a physical keyboard versus double tapping the up arrow on a tablet. Or using 'Ctrl' on a Windows keyboard versus 'Command' on a Mac.

Navigation

The activities can be completed using an external mouse, trackpad, or touchscreen. Learners will see the instructions 'Click or tap' in their Student's Books and have time to practise their navigation skills as they work through the activities.

Chapter 1 – Our digital world
Project: Design a robot to help someone who works at your school

Chapter overview

In this chapter, learners will explore the technology in the world around them with a focus on the school community. They will then speak to the users of technology in their community and design a robot to help them with an everyday task.

	Chapter 1: Lesson summary	
Lesson	**Learning Objectives**	**Summary**
1	• Identify a range of personal computers in our digital world, including desktop computers, laptops, tablets and smartphones • State the functions of a range of computer systems, including communication, entertainment, creativity and for smart devices • List a range of programs a computer can run, including games, apps and content creation tools	Learners identify different kinds of computer from everyday life and identify objects that are not computers. They learn that computers run programs, including games, apps and content creation tools such as a drawing app or word processor.
2	• Identify everyday devices that use computers to control what they do, and the tasks they do in our digital world • Define 'robot' and state common tasks that they perform in our digital world	Learners identify everyday digital devices that contain computers. They learn that robots can perform tasks and may be able to move or listen and talk.
3	• Determine the common tasks that a person from the local community performs	Learners create a list of questions to ask a community guest about the everyday tasks that they perform in their job. They carry out an interview with the guest.
4	• Identify common tasks that a robot could perform	Using the interview answers from the previous lesson, learners identify tasks that a robot could perform to help their guest.
5	• Design a robot that will perform an everyday task	Learners design their own robots to perform an everyday task to help their guest.
6	• Showcase a robot design	Learners complete a showcase of their robot designs to an audience.

End of chapter project	Design a robot to help someone who works at your school
Example ideas that learners could design:	  

Chapter 1 – Our digital world

Project: Design a robot to help someone who works at your school

Name	

	Working towards (1)	Meets expected (2)	Exceeding expected (3)	Score
Sketches	• Minimal sketches of robot design/s have been created	• Some good sketches of robot designs have been created	• Detailed sketches of the robot designs have been created	
Final design	• A partially complete sketch of the final robot design has been created	• A complete sketch of the final robot design has been created, the robot is described well (verbally or through labels)	• A detailed sketch of the final robot design has been created, the robot is explained well (verbally or through labels)	
Everyday task	• The task that the robot is designed to perform is not related to the needs of the guest the class is helping	• The task that the robot is designed to perform is related to the needs of the guest the class is helping	• The task that the robot is designed to perform goes above and beyond the needs of the guest	

Teacher feedback	
Learner response	

Chapter 1:	Lesson 1 Computers around you

Learning Objectives	<ul><li>Identify a range of personal computers in our digital world, including desktop computers, laptops, tablets and smartphones</li><li>State the functions of a range of computer systems, including communication, entertainment, creativity and for smart devices</li><li>List a range of programs a computer can run, including games, apps and content creation tools</li></ul>
New key terms	**computer** – electronic machine that can perform tasks **app (program)** – used for specific tasks on a computer

You will need	<ul><li>Pre-identify some examples of computers in your classroom that you could point out to learners.</li><li>**Optional:** Bring examples of computers from the wider school into your classroom.</li></ul>	**Key pedagogy**	Classroom talk

Activity	Instructions	Guidance
1	<ul><li>Introduce the definition of computer (📖 Page 2).</li><li>Use the images as examples of different types of computer.</li><li>Use Discuss 1 (📖 Page 2).</li></ul>	<ul><li>Before the lesson, identify some examples of computers in your classroom that you can point out to learners; for example, a laptop or desktop computer.</li><li>Mention or show that computers come in different shapes and sizes. A smartphone is a computer that fits in your pocket!</li><li>Bring examples of computers from the wider school into your classroom. Focus on common devices, such as smartphones and tablets, as not everyone owns a traditional desktop computer.</li></ul>
2	<ul><li>Ask learners to complete (📖 Page 1) Task A, 'Which is not a computer?'. Learners circle the images that are not a computer.</li></ul>	<ul><li>Move around the class and check answers. Point out where learners can find the definition of a computer in the Workbook and show them that computers are electronic machines.</li></ul>

Activity	Instructions	Guidance
3	• Ask learners to look at the illustrations of activities performed with computers (📖 Page 3). • Use Discuss 2 (📖 Page 2).	• Draw on examples of when learners have used computers to perform an activity at school; for example, to watch something during an assembly or to read from an electronic device.
4	• Ask learners to complete (📖 Page 2) Task B , 'I use a computer to…'.' Learners draw a picture to show how they like to use a computer.	• Point out the example illustrations in the Workbook. Explain the activities along with the type of computer in each illustration. • Uses of computers can be categorised as: communication, entertainment, creativity and for smart devices. • You could tell the class a way that you like to use a computer.
5	• Recap the definition of app and ask learners to look at the illustrations of computer programs (📖 Page 3). • Use Discuss 3 (📖 Page 3). • Explain that learners should make sure that games are appropriate for their age group, and that they should ask an adult if they are allowed to play it.	• Example programs could include popular games on smartphones or games consoles. They could also include programs that you have used in the classroom such as a phonics program or eBook. • Mention that apps on a phone or tablet are programs.
6	• Discuss whether learners were surprised to find out that tablets and smartphones are computers. • Repeat the key terms 'computer' and 'app (program)' with their definitions. • Remind the class of the great examples of computer programs that they gave.	• As this is the first time learners are using these books, you could point out useful features like where to find the key terms in both the Student's Book and Workbook.

Build on this: Demonstrate the programs that your computers have in your school environment. Have they used them before? Do they recognise them? Can they guess what they might do from the icon?

Chapter 1: Lesson 2 Computers inside devices and robots

Learning Objectives	• Identify everyday devices that use computers to control what they do, and the tasks they do in our digital world • Define 'robot' and state common tasks that they perform in our digital world
New key terms	**digital device** – object that contains a small computer to perform tasks **robot** – digital device that performs a useful task on its own; it may be able to move or talk

You will need	• Pre-plan a tour of the school or local community to spot devices that use computers to control what they do and, if possible, devices that use robotics. • Take photos of examples of devices and robots that learners will be familiar with but will not be able to access during the lesson.	**Key pedagogy**	Classroom talk

Activity	Instructions	Guidance
1	• Introduce the definition of digital device (📖 Page 3). • Use the images as examples of different types of digital device. Highlight the tasks they complete. • Use Discuss 4 (📖 Page 4).	• If there are any words you use locally to refer to devices (for example, gadget), make the connection for your learners. • Examples of digital devices include a remote-controlled car toy, a microwave oven or an electronic till in a supermarket. Use examples that will be familiar to your learners.
2	• Introduce the definition of robot (📖 Page 5). • Use the images as examples of different types of robot. • Use Discuss 5 (📖 Page 5).	• Have you read any stories, as a class, that include robots or are there any TV programs or films that include robots? You could use these to make a connection to the learning. • Make sure you highlight robots that do not look like people; for example, robots that are used in a factory assembling cars.

3	• Tell the class that they will now go on a tour of the school (or local environment) to spot any digital devices and robots. • If you cannot take the class on a tour, identify digital devices in the images (📖 Page 5) and use Discuss 6 (📖 Page 5). • Learners should bring their Workbooks on the tour. They will log what they see as they go along in (📖 Pages 3 and 4) Task A, 'Digital devices and robots around you'.	• Pre-plan a tour of your school or local environment. Select which digital devices, and potentially robots, you want learners to spot. • At each location take the time to ask learners what tasks they think the devices perform. Give them time to record what they have seen in their Workbooks. • Alternatively, guide the class through the three images in the Student's Book and direct them to record what they see in their Workbooks.
4	• Repeat the key terms 'digital device' and 'robot' with their definitions. • Ask for examples of digital devices and then robots. • Encourage learners to notice examples of digital devices or robots in their everyday life.	• Select some Workbooks to show to the class to remind learners of the examples they found. • Did learners point out any devices that weren't digital or robotic along the way? If so, you could address that now and reinforce why they aren't digital devices.

Build on this: **Using your class bookshelf or school library, find books that mention digital devices or robots. Do learners know of any other books that include examples?**

Chapter 1:	Lesson 3 Interview a guest		
Learning Objective	• Determine the common tasks that a person from the local community performs		
New key terms	**interview** – a discussion with a person, where you ask questions to find things out		
You will need	• A guest who works in the school and can be available during the lesson • **Optional:** A tablet, phone or video camera to record the interview	**Key pedagogy**	Design thinking

Activity	Instructions	Guidance
1	• Introduce the project brief of designing a robot to help someone who works in the school.	• Don't spend too much time on the project brief. Learners will be interviewing a guest before they start designing their robot.
2	• Learners are going to need to find out how they can help someone from their community. Go through the example of a school meal supervisor who serves food to learners (📖 Page 6). • Use Discuss 7 (📖 Page 7).	• Relate the example to a locally relevant example of someone who helps to provide food in your school.

3	• Announce that you will be interviewing someone in the school community (📖 Page 7).
	• Tell learners who you will be interviewing.
	• Use Discuss 8 (📖 Page 7).
	• Write down learners' suggestions in a list.
		• Create some excitement about who you will be interviewing.
		• Encourage empathy so learners want to help the person you have chosen.
		• Talk to the guest before the lesson about the project so they can give useful answers.
		• If you are unable to bring in a special guest, you could role-play a person in the school and come up with some answers that would support the project brief.
		• Sample questions to help guide the discussion:
		  • What everyday tasks do you do in your job?
		  • Which tasks take the longest?
		  • Are any jobs repetitive?
		  • Are any tasks difficult for one person to do?

4	• Explain to learners that they need to make notes from the interview (📖 Pages 5 and 6) Task A, 'The interview'. • Introduce your guest and invite learners to take turns asking the questions from the list the class created. • Give learners time to complete their notes in their Workbooks.	• Make your own notes to help your learners remember the answers the guest gives during the interview. • You could record the interview with a microphone or video if your guest agrees.

Activity	Instructions	Guidance
5	<ul><li>Repeat the word 'interview' with its definition (📖 Page 6).</li><li>Use Discuss 9 (📖 Page 7).</li><li>Remind learners that their project is to design a robot to help a community member.</li><li>Explain that the answers to their interview questions will help them to design a useful robot to help their guest.</li><li>Ask 'What have you learned about asking questions and listening to other people?'</li></ul>	<ul><li>Use examples from (📖✏ Pages 5 and 6) Task A, 'The interview' during the discussion.</li><li>You can use the guidance from Activity 3 again to support this.</li><li>Encourage learners to think about the needs of their guest.</li></ul>

Build on this: Ask learners to think about a robot that you have discussed in Lesson 2. Discuss the questions that the inventor of the robot would have needed to ask the people who the robot helps.

Chapter 1:	Lesson 4 How could a robot help?		
Learning Objective	• Identify common tasks that a robot could perform		
You will need	<ul><li>The answers to the questions that learners recorded in their Workbooks in Lesson 3</li><li>**Optional:** Video or sound recordings from the interview</li></ul>	**Key pedagogy**	Design thinking

Activity	Instructions	Guidance
1	<ul><li>Go through the examples (📖 Page 8) to show common tasks that a robot can perform.</li><li>Use Discuss 10 (📖 Page 8).</li></ul>	<ul><li>Robots are generally good at tasks that are repetitive, require speed and are boring. They can also go to dangerous areas (perhaps where height is involved at a school).</li></ul>
2	<ul><li>Ask learners to revisit the interview activity from the previous lesson (📖✏ Pages 5 and 6), Task A, 'The interview'.</li><li>Use Discuss 11 (📖 Page 9).</li><li>Use Discuss 12 (📖 Page 9).</li><li>Split the class into small groups and ask them to generate ideas of what a robot could do to help their guest.</li></ul>	<ul><li>Give learners time to remind themselves of the tasks they recorded in their Workbooks.</li><li>If you recorded the interview, you could play clips back to learners as a reminder.</li><li>Use your own interview notes as prompts.</li></ul>

Activity	Instructions	Guidance
3	• Explain that learners need to choose a task that a robot could complete to help their guest, then write or draw how the guest currently completes that task (📖✏ Pages 7 and 8) Task A, 'Choose a task to help your guest with'.	• Some learners may need guiding towards tasks that would be suitable for a robot. • If learners are struggling to decide which task their robot could perform, revisit the answers from the guest and support them with finding an appropriate task.
4	• Use Discuss 13 (📖 Page 9).	• Show some examples from Workbooks to the class. • Link examples to tasks that robots are good at and tasks that would help the guest.

Build on this: **Learners could work in pairs to provide feedback on their chosen task.**

Chapter 1:	Lesson 5 Design your robot		
Learning Objective	• Design a robot that will perform an everyday task		
You will need	• Coloured pencils and crayons for learners to add colour to their designs	**Key pedagogy**	Get creative

Activity	Instructions	Guidance
1	• Read the project brief. Tell learners that they are now going to design their robot to help someone who works at their school. (📖 Page 10) • Talk through the example illustrations and the help they provide. • Use Discuss 14 (📖 Page 10).	• Some learners might work better in a pair when being creative. Use your discretion to allocate pairs if needed. • If learners need a reminder of the task they chose, they should look back at (📖✏ Pages 7 and 8) Task A, 'Choose a task to help your guest with'.

Activity	Instructions	Guidance
2	• Give learners time to sketch ideas for their robot (📖 Page 9) Task A, 'Sketch your robot ideas'.	• Encourage learners to sketch multiple ideas for their robot before choosing one to take forwards. They could combine their favourite parts from different sketches or try completely new sketches each time. • You could model this on a whiteboard as an additional way of supporting learners.
3	• Give learners time to design their final robot (📖 Page 10) Task B, 'Draw your final design'.	• Explain that learners will be showcasing their designs in the next lesson, so they should fill the page as much as possible, using colour and even labels.

Build on this: If there is time, learners can work in pairs to provide feedback on their designs and see if they can add any improvements to what they have done.

Chapter 1:	Lesson 6 Showcase your robot		
Learning Objective	• Showcase a robot design		
New key terms	**showcase** – present a project to an audience		
You will need	• The robot designs that learners created in Lesson 5 in their Workbooks	**Key pedagogy**	Showcase

Activity	Instructions	Guidance
1	• Introduce the definition of showcase (📖 Page 11) and explain that learners will now be showcasing their final robot designs. • Run through the tips for showcasing.	• Use the illustration (📖 Page 11) to show how a whole-class showcase might look. • Draw specific attention to how the tips are represented in the illustration, especially the power of using pictures. • If time allows, encourage learners to practise with a partner.

Activity	Instructions	Guidance
2	• Complete the showcase activity (📖 Page 11).	• You could split the class into groups to showcase to each other. • Encourage learners to watch others closely to get tips for showcasing and to pick their favourite idea.
3	• Ask learners to complete (📖✏ Page 11) Task A, 'Reflection'. They should answer the two reflection questions by colouring in the stars. Guide learners with the task by explaining that colouring five stars is positive and one star is weak. • Use Reflection (📖 Page 12) in pairs or small groups.	• Focus on the importance of robots helping humans. • Celebrate how much work has gone into creating and showcasing their designs. • Mention that reflecting helps you to remember what you have learned.
Build on this: **Give learners time to ask each other questions about their designs.**		

Chapter 2 – Content creation

Project: Design and build an app that feeds a character their favourite foods

Chapter overview

In this chapter, learners will explore password security and how to log on and off from a computer. They will then build their digital skills by practising dragging and dropping, scrolling and typing. They will use these skills to select foods for a character in an app to eat.

Chapter 2: Lesson summary		
Lesson	Learning Objectives	Summary
1	• State what a password is and why a password is useful • Switch on and log onto a computer using a password	Learners discover what a password is, what makes a good password, and why they are important. They then practise logging on and off from the school computers.
2	• Make design decisions for an app	Learners are introduced to the 'Feed Frank' project and decide which three foods they want their app to use. They learn about capital and lowercase letters.
3	• Use a physical or digital keyboard to enter familiar words into a word processor • Use modifier keys (for example, caps lock) on a physical or digital keyboard	Learners practise typing using either a physical or a digital keyboard (depending on your equipment). They learn about typing capital and lowercase letters.
4	• Save and open documents • Use click, scroll and swipe to interact with a computer	Learners take their first look at Scratch and discover how to change the costumes of a sprite for their Feed Frank app.
5	• Save and open documents • Use click, drag, drop, scroll and swipe to interact with a computer	Learners play with the app and practise their digital skills by typing, dragging and dropping.
6	• Save and open documents • Use click, drag, drop, scroll and swipe to interact with a computer	Learners showcase their apps to the class and reflect on how well their project went.

End of chapter project	Design and build an app that feeds a character their favourite foods
Example ideas that learners could design:	

Chapter 2 – Content creation

Project: Design and build an app that feeds a character their favourite foods

Name	

	Working towards (1)	Meets expected (2)	Exceeding expected (3)	Score
Sketches	• Three foods were chosen for the 'Feed Frank' app	• The names of the three chosen foods were written down	• The names of the three chosen foods were written down, spelled correct, with a capital letter at the beginning of all words	
Final design	• The 'Feed Frank' app still uses the default foods, indicating that choices may not have been selected	• The 'Feed Frank' app uses the chosen food costumes	• The 'Feed Frank' app uses the chosen food costumes and the learner could explain why they chose them	
Everyday task	• The learner could type some of the words correctly	• The learner could type all of the words correctly, with some use of capital letters	• The learner could type all of the words correctly, using a capital letter at the beginning of each word	

Teacher feedback	
Learner response	

Chapter 2:	Lesson 1 Passwords			
Learning Objectives	• State what a password is and why a password is useful • Switch on and log onto a computer using a password			
New key terms	**password –** secret code you use to keep your information safe **log on –** entering a username and password to use a computer **username –** personal name you use to access your information, for example to use a computer at school **log off –** exiting a computer when you have finished using it			
You will need	• Usernames and passwords for all your learners	**Key pedagogy**		Develop practical skills

Activity	Instructions	Guidance
1	• Introduce the chapter to learners and the project that they are working towards (📖 Page 13).	• The project will involve learners choosing three food items to feed a character. They will then run the program and it will ask them to type the names of each food. • Remind learners of the definition of an app.
2	• Introduce the concept of a password to your learners (📖 Page 14). They might have seen a password being entered before. The example illustrations might help learners remember this. • Use Discuss 1 (📖 Page 14). • Use Discuss 2 (📖 Page 14.	• Learners might have seen an adult enter a PIN into a smartphone or an ATM, or type a password to log into a computer. • Discussion 2 should lead learners to thinking about using a password to log on to the computers at school.
3	• Introduce the concept of a 'good password' (📖 Page 14). It is a good idea to use three random words for a password.	• National Cyber Security Centres recommend that users have a password that contains three random words (visit a National Cyber Security Centre website and search for 'top tips for staying secure online'). This makes a password difficult to guess but easier for the user to remember.

Activity	Instructions	Guidance

4	• Ask learners to complete (📖 Page 12) Task A, 'Three random pictures'. Learners should think of three pictures that they can draw to help them remember a password made of three random words.
	  • Remind learners to not write the word 'password' alongside their three images, to keep it as safe as possible within the context of the task!
	  • Use a whiteboard (or equivalent) to produce an example drawing for learners, e.g. Fish Cloud Egg.
		• If learners need further support with this, point out common objects around the classroom or computer room, or things outside the window.
		• Encourage learners to draw pictures of things that they can spell.
		• You could encourage them to write the word but this should come with a warning that somebody might be able to use their password if it was written down.

5	• Introduce the definitions of log on and log off (📖 Page 15), using the illustrations as support. • Demonstrate how to log on and log off from the computers in your school. If your computers load quite quickly, you could also ask learners to switch on their computers themselves before they log on. • Repeat the process many times to give learners practice with this skill. It can take some time for them to get used to this.	• You will need to follow your school policy when demonstrating how to log on and off from the school computers. • You could create a step-by-step sheet to have out on the desk to support learners with logging on and off. • If learners can create their own passwords that are linked to their usernames, you can use the three random words from the Workbooks to support this. Remind them not to share this information.
6	• Ask learners to practise writing the new key terms they have learned, (📖 Page 13) Task B, 'Key terms practice'.	
7	• Use Discuss 3 (📖 Page 15).	• Check that learners know what a good password is.

Build on this: **Ask learners to explain to a partner why it is important to keep a password secret.**

Chapter 2:	Lesson 2 Make a choice
Learning Objective	• Make design decisions for an app
New key terms	**capital letters** – big letters that we use at the start of a sentence or a name. Capital letters are bigger than lowercase letters.

	lowercase letters – smaller letters that we use most of the time when we write and type. Lowercase letters are smaller than capital letters.		
You will need	• **Optional:** Scrap paper, mini whiteboards	**Key pedagogy**	Get creative

Activity	Instructions	Guidance
1	• Remind learners that the project for this chapter is to design and build an app that feeds a character their favourite foods. • Show learners the ten food items that they can choose to 'Feed Frank', using the images (📖 Page 16). • Use Discuss 4 (📖 Page 16).	• Give learners some time to look at the images and make their choices. • They could talk to a partner about their decision.
2	• Ask learners to complete (📓 Page 14) Task A, 'Choose three foods'. Learners circle the three foods that they have chosen.	• Note that the images in the Workbook are in black and white, so may appear different from the ones in the Student's Books.
3	• Use the description to explain to learners the difference between a capital letter and a lowercase letter (📖 Page 17). • Use Discuss 5 (📖 Page 17) in reference to the capital T and the lowercase t.	• You could link this to your literacy/English lessons. • You could demonstrate this on a whiteboard (or equivalent). • If you have mini whiteboards for your learners, they could practise writing capital and lowercase letters before moving to the Workbooks.
4	• Ask learners to complete (📓 Page 15) Task B, 'Write your food words' and practise writing their chosen three food words. • Remind them to use a capital letter at the beginning of each word.	• Provide additional scrap paper for learners that might need more practice.
5	• Write a series of capital letters and lowercase letters on the whiteboard (or equivalent). • Ask learners to tell you whether the letters are lowercase or capitals.	• Learners can practise this further on scrap paper or mini whiteboards.

Build on this: Learners could count the number of capital letters that they can spot around the classroom.

Chapter 2:	Lesson 3 Type your words

Learning Objectives	• Use a physical or digital keyboard to enter familiar words into a word processor • Use modifier keys (for example Shift and Caps Lock) on a physical or digital keyboard		
New key terms	**word processor** – a program you use to type words into a computer to create a document		
You will need	• Workbooks with learners' three food words listed • Computers set up with a word processor on the screen for typing practice (if you don't think there is time for them to log on and off themselves)	**Key pedagogy**	Develop practical skills

Activity	Instructions	Guidance
1	• Introduce definition of word processor (📖 Page 18). • Explain to learners that they will be using a word processor today to type in some words. • Explain the purpose of the 'caps lock' button on a keyboard. The cartoon strip helps to demonstrate this. • Use Discuss 6 (📖 Page 18).	• A quick hands-up response to discussion 6 would be appropriate here.
2	• Demonstrate using 'caps lock' on your school computers. • Give learners a few minutes to practise typing capital and lowercase letters.	• You could use this time as another opportunity to practise logging on and off if your learners were quick at doing this in Lesson 1. However, it is more important that they get time to practise typing. • Your keyboards might not have a 'caps lock' button. If they are digital keyboards, you can usually access 'caps lock' by double-tapping the 'Shift' key.

Activity	Instructions	Guidance
3	• Use the images (📖 Page 19) to remind learners that in the previous lesson they chose three food items for their project. • Remind learners of the previous task from Lesson 3 (📖✏ Page 15) where they wrote their three foods.	• If learners missed the previous lesson, they can choose their three food items now. They could type the words by copying them from the Student's Book (📖 Page 19).
4	• Demonstrate how to type some of the food words into a word processor. Reinforce the use of a capital letters at the beginning of each word. • Instruct learners to type out their three food words into the word processor. • They should type it as many times as they can, working to increase their speed and confidence through practice.	• You don't need to go through every food item on the list; three food items is probably sufficient at this stage.
5	• After allowing time for learners to practise their typing skills, ask them to complete Task A (📖✏ Page 16), 'Find the capital letters'. Learners find and circle all the capital letters on the page.	• If you have a visualiser (a camera that projects on the screen), you could show the answers to learners on the big screen. • If you do not have a visualiser, you could write the answers on a whiteboard (or equivalent).

Build on this: Learners could type the alphabet into the word processor. They should try to remember the correct order. You could provide an alphabet to support this, or point to a classroom display if you have one.

Chapter 2:	Lesson 4 Select foods in Scratch		
Learning Objectives	• Save and open documents • Use click, scroll and swipe to interact with a computer		
New key terms	**Scratch** – program that allows you to create your own programs or apps **open** – view a file on a computer **save** – save a file on a computer so that you can use it again next time **sprite** – character or object in Scratch **stage** – area in Scratch where you can play with your app **costume** – different options for how your sprite looks in Scratch; it is like the clothes you wear each day		
You will need	• Computers that can run Scratch (see Software section of this Teacher's Guide for more information) • The Scratch starter project 'Feed Frank' (Website C2L4R1) • The food choices that learners decided in their Workbooks	**Key pedagogy**	Get creative

Activity	Instructions	Guidance
1	• Introduce the Scratch program to your learners (📖 Page 20). • Demonstrate Scratch on a computer or tablet. • Reinforce to learners that Scratch is a program. • Use Discuss 7 (📖 Page 20).	• Learners may have used Scratch at home with a parent or older sibling. They may have used ScratchJr on a tablet or smartphone at home. • You could play the Scratch trailer video on the Scratch home page to introduce Scratch to learners (Website C2L4R2).
2	• Introduce the definition of open and demonstrate how to 'open' the 'Feed Frank' project in Scratch (📖 Page 20).	• See the teacher guidance section at the beginning of this Teacher's Guide to learn about the different ways that you can use Scratch in your school. • Link to Scratch project: (Website C2L4R1) • This is another opportunity to practise logging on to the school computers if you feel that learners will do this without taking up too much lesson time.

Activity	Instructions	Guidance
3	• Introduce the term save (📖 Page 21). • Tell learners that it is important to save their work frequently in case something happens to their computer. We use 'save' to avoid losing our work. • Demonstrate how to 'save' in Scratch.	• See the teacher guidance at the beginning of this Teacher's Guide to learn about the different ways to save a file in Scratch.
4	• Show learners the Scratch layout (📖 Page 21). They should see the three areas: the Editor, the Sprites and the Stage. • Now ask them to look closely at the Sprites area. Ask, 'Can you spot the three food sprites and Frank?'	• They can spot the sprites either in the image in the Student's Book or directly on their computers.
5	• Introduce the term costumes using the description (📖 Page 21) and the complete definition (📖 Page 20). • Use the steps for picking the correct costume for each food item (📖 Page 22). Demonstrate to learners how to change the costume of each food sprite. • Point out to learners that they can check whether they have chosen the correct costume by looking in the 'Sprite' area. • Instruct learners to save their work.	• Provide additional mouse support if this is new to learners. You can adjust the mouse setting to increase the size of the pointer and to slow it down to make it easier for young people to use the tool. Speak to a technician for support with this if needed. • Make sure learners have saved their projects to use in the next lesson.
6	• Ask learners to complete (📖 Page 17) Task A, 'Scratch quiz'. Learners answer questions about their knowledge so far of Scratch.	• This could be set as homework if there is limited time during the lesson.

Build on this: If learners choose their food items quickly, they can go into the 'Frank' sprite and choose a different costume for Frank to change the way he stands. They could also support any learners in the class who need extra help.

Chapter 2:	Lesson 5 Play your Scratch game		
Learning Objectives	• Save and open documents • Use click, drag, drop, scroll and swipe to interact with a computer		
You will need	• The saved projects from Lesson 4	**Key pedagogy**	Get creative

Activity	Instructions	Guidance
1	• Demonstrate how to find the Scratch projects from the previous lesson and support learners with finding their work.	• Read the guidance at the beginning of this Teacher's Guide regarding saving and loading Scratch projects. • Having 'digital leaders' in the classroom who are good at helping others would be helpful. They can provide extra support in getting the projects loaded.
2	• Demonstrate how to play with the Feed Frank app and guide learners through the steps (📖 Pages 23 and 24). • Show learners how to click on the green flag to start the game. • Remind learners how to type on the keyboard. Ask them to type the correct name of their chosen food in the box and click 'Enter'. • Show learners how to drag and drop the food items to feed Frank.	• You might want to break this down into several small steps to make it easier for learners to remember your instructions. • The instructions on how to play the game are also shown on pages 23 and 24 of the Student's Book. Learners can use this as additional support.

3	• An important part of this activity is giving learners time to practise these digital skills:
	  • typing
	  • using 'caps lock'
	  • dragging and dropping.
	• After demonstrating how to play the game, give learners plenty of time to continue playing the game and to practise the above skills.
		• Provide additional demonstrations and reminders if learners need extra support. You could ask them to support each other in pairs.

4	• Learners have been developing their digital skills in this lesson. Ask learners to rate their skills (📖 Page 18) Task A, 'Rate your progress'. Learners read the 'I can' statement and colour in the graphics to show how they rate themselves. If they colour all five, they are very confident and agree with the statement. If they only colour one, they do not agree with the statement.	• Read the questions aloud to the class to support with reading. • Observe learners when they are rating themselves. Some learners will underestimate how good they are at a skill and give themselves a low score. If you have observed them doing better, encourage them to provide a higher rating for themselves. Point out the positive things they have done and remind them of what they have achieved.

Activity	Instructions	Guidance

Build on this: Learners can change their mind about the foods that they want to feed Frank. They can go back into the Costumes tab and change the food items.

Chapter 2:	Lesson 6 Showcase your app		
Learning Objectives	• Save and open documents • Use click, drag, drop, scroll and swipe to interact with a computer		
You will need	• The saved projects from Lesson 5	**Key pedagogy**	Get creative

Activity	Instructions	Guidance
1	• Demonstrate how to find the Scratch projects from the previous lesson and support learners with finding their work.	• Read the guidance at the beginning of the Teacher's Guide regarding saving and loading Scratch projects. • Having 'digital leaders' in the classroom who are good at helping others would be helpful. They can provide extra support in getting the projects loaded.
2	• Ask learners to think about what they will say when they showcase their app and talk through the suggestions (📖 Page 25).	• It is important that learners get used to practising how they are going to showcase to others to build their confidence in public speaking.
3	• Split the class into two groups. • The first group will stand by their own computers with their app on the screen and showcase it to the second group. • After each person has shown their app to three people, swap the groups over.	• There are lots of different ways to showcase apps to the class, whether your class is large or small. Read the showcase guidance at the start of this Teacher's Guide for more ideas.
4	• Ask learners to reflect on the lesson (📖 Page 19) Task A, 'Reflection'. Learners should colour all five stars for a positive rating and one star for a weak rating.	• Read the questions aloud to the class to support with reading.

Activity	Instructions	Guidance
5	• Take a moment to celebrate learners' achievements, using the 'congratulations' page (📖 Page 26). • Reflection: Ask learners to discuss or think about 'How did it feel to showcase your app to other learners in the class?'	

Build on this: Learners might have received some feedback about their app during their showcase. If they did, they could use additional time to improve their app. If they need further practice with their digital skills, they could choose to spend time doing this instead.

Chapter 3 – Create with code 1

Project: Plan a journey for a Bee-Bot to take to tell a story

Chapter overview

In this chapter, learners will discover what an algorithm is. They will follow an algorithm for an everyday task. They will then learn about directional instructions and enter code into a Bee-Bot to follow a path. For their projects, they will plan a unique journey for their Bee-Bot that follows a story.

Chapter 3: Lesson summary		
Lesson	Learning Objectives	Summary
1	• Define the term 'algorithm' • Follow a sequence for an everyday task	Learners use discussion and role play to explore algorithms and understand the importance of clear, ordered instructions.
2	• State simple instructions to navigate a path using directions • State that algorithms can be recreated as code on computers • Translate an algorithm into program code	Learners are introduced to the Bee-Bot floor robot. They turn algorithms into code and enter the code into the Bee-Bot. They practise using a Bee-Bot to follow paths.
3	• Predict what is likely to happen when code runs • Run and test code	Learners explore the term 'predict' and make predictions based on information they already know. They enter code into Bee-Bots to test their predictions and make changes for their Bee-Bots to reach objects.
4	• Create a sequence to navigate a story	Learners explore an example story with code for reaching three objects. They choose three objects for their own story and write down the order.
5	• Write code to navigate a story • Run and test code that navigates a story	Learners place their objects and starting point on the floor. They predict, test and refine code for reaching one object at a time. They run through their whole story from start to finish.
6	• Showcase code that navigates a story	Learners share their story and talk through their code before reflecting on the project.

End of chapter project	Plan a journey for a Bee-Bot to take to tell a story
Example ideas that learners could design:	  

Chapter 3 – Create with code 1

Project: Plan a journey for a Bee-Bot to take to tell a story

Name	

	Working towards (1)	Meets expected (2)	Exceeding expected (3)	Score
Sketches	• There were less than three objects and/or the objects were not built into the story	• There were three objects that made sense in the story	• There were more than three objects that made sense in the story	
Final design	• The code used didn't move the Bee-Bot to all the objects and/or went to the objects in the wrong order	• The code moved the Bee-Bot to each object in the correct order	• The code moved the Bee-Bot to each object in the correct order	
Everyday task	• Didn't participate in the showcase	• Helped to tell the story during the showcase. Talked about the code and any problems that were fixed	• Helped to tell the story during the showcase. Talked about the code, any problems that were fixed and used props to help tell the story.	

Teacher feedback	
Learner response	

Chapter 3:	Lesson 1 Everyday algorithms		
Learning Objectives	<ul><li>Define the term 'algorithm'</li><li>Follow a sequence for an everyday task</li></ul>		
New key terms	algorithm – set of instructions to complete a task or solve a problem		
You will need	<ul><li>Several copies of the class register so that you can demonstrate, and learners can role-play, the process without impacting actual learner attendance figures</li></ul>	Key pedagogy	Role play

Activity	Instructions	Guidance
1	<ul><li>Use the description to define 'algorithm' (📖 Page 28).</li><li>Use Discuss 1 (📖 Page 28).</li><li>Use the storyboard to talk through the instructions for taking a class register.</li><li>Explain the importance of the order of instructions in an algorithm using the second storyboard.</li><li>Use Discuss 2 (📖 Page 28).</li><li>Use Discuss 3 (📖 Page 28).</li></ul>	<ul><li>Learners follow instructions when they play a playground game or board game. Provide familiar examples from the classroom.</li><li>The storyboard might not match the exact way you take your class register but is just an example of the task at this stage.</li><li>The correct order for the steps would be 1, 3, 2. The problem with the order shown is that the teacher could mark learners present or absent when that is not the case, so they would not know who is in the class that day.</li></ul>
2	<ul><li>Ask learners to complete (📖 Page 20) Task A, 'Key term algorithm'. Learners practise writing the new key term 'algorithm'.</li></ul>	<ul><li>As algorithm is a key term that learners will be unfamiliar with, take this opportunity to get learners to become familiar with the word.</li><li>You could put up a piece of paper with this new key term on it or get learners to practise saying it aloud.</li></ul>

Activity	Instructions	Guidance
3	• Demonstrate the process you go through when taking the class register (📖 Page 29). Ask learners to watch you and think about the steps and order of steps. • Use Discuss 4 (📖 Page 29). • Write the answers on the board to build an algorithm together for taking the class register. Change the order and develop the instructions as you discuss the process together.	• You might need to demonstrate the process several times or streamline it if you have a complex or electronic system for taking the class register. • Encourage learners to think about the tasks and the order as they discuss the instructions. You will probably find that some steps are missing initially, so need to be added in or moved around to create the final algorithm.
4	• Tell the class that they will be role-playing taking the class register and will be following their algorithm in the order it is written on the board. • Split the class into small groups and give each group a copy of the register. The groups should decide who will be the teacher, who will play the learners and who will read out the instructions one step at a time.	• Give learners time to practise the role play a few times. You could encourage them to change roles to practise giving and interpreting instructions. • Observe the role plays and provide support. As the scenario is acted out, make a note of instructions that could be clearer, were missing or were in the wrong order.
5	• Use Discuss 5 (📖 Page 29). Make any required changes to the algorithm on the board. • Ask learners to complete (📖 Page 21) Task B, 'Reflection'. Learners reflect on the class register algorithm and how the order of an algorithm is important.	• Check learners' reflection statements and monitor participation in discussion. Pay particular attention to where learners found the role play helped to highlight instructions that were missing, in the wrong order or could be clearer.

Build on this: Learners could storyboard their algorithm for taking the class register with each frame on a different piece of paper. They could then assemble them in different orders to think through the problems created in each scenario.

Chapter 3:	Lesson 2 Bee-Bot paths		
Learning Objectives	• State simple instructions to navigate a path using directions • State that algorithms can be recreated as code on computers • Translate an algorithm to program code		
New key terms	**code** – instructions that tell a computer what to do **Bee-Bot** – robot that uses code to move in different directions		
You will need	• Enough Bee-Bots to give one each to small groups of learners • If you do not have Bee-Bots, you could use a Code & Go robot mouse or similar directional floor robot. • If you do not have access to floor robots, you can adapt this chapter to use an online simulator (search online for the Bee-Bot terrapin logo website). • Make sure your Bee-Bots have batteries or are charged.	**Key pedagogy**	Physical computing

Activity	Instructions	Guidance
1	• Use the description to define 'code' (📖 Page 30). • Introduce learners to the Bee-Bot by walking through the storyboard cartoon. • Use Discuss 6 (📖 Page 30).	• Draw attention to the movement of the Bee-Bot in the cartoon to show how the arrows relate to the movement shown in the images. • You could act this out as you talk through the storyboard frames.
2	• Take one of your physical Bee-Bots and show it to learners. • Use the illustration to show where the buttons are on the Bee-Bot (📖 Page 31). • Code the Bee-Bot to re-enact the path shown in the cartoon (📖 Page 30).	• Press forwards, right, forwards, forwards, left, go. • Make a mistake when entering the code (or clear the program at the end) to show learners how to clear the code from the Bee-Bot. • Draw particular attention to the changes in direction as learners may expect the Bee-Bot to move and turn, not just turn. • You could draw the path on a large sheet of paper (each square should be 15cm × 15cm).

3	• Ask learners to complete (📖✏ Page 22) Task A, 'Follow a path'. • Ask, 'Where is the Bee-Bot positioned at the end and in which direction is it facing?'	• Learners should use a pencil to follow the path. Explain that one forwards move will move the Bee-Bot forwards one grid square. • Observe learners completing the activity. Learners might need reminding that the left and right buttons rotate the Bee-Bot but do not move it forwards in that direction.
4	• Ask learners to code their Bee-Bots to navigate the paths (📖 Page 31). • Use Discuss 7 (📖 Page 31).	• Remind learners that they can clear their code if they make a mistake or want to start a new path. • This activity is to get learners used to using the buttons to input sequences of directional code. You could use floor grids to move along but it is not necessary. • Make sure the Bee-Bots are turned on for learners.
5	• Ask learners to complete (📖✏ Page 23) Task B, 'Create a path'. • Use Discuss 8 (📖 Page 31).	• Observe learners creating their algorithms. Encourage them to use all the buttons to familiarise themselves with what they do. • Learners can create more than one short path, or one long path. • Check that learners understand that they can clear their code if they realise they have made a mistake. If they realise after running their code, they can start again with new code.

Build on this: Learners can swap Workbooks to practise their coding skills with algorithms that have been created by others.

Chapter 3:	Lesson 3 Predict and run

Learning Objectives	• Predict what is likely to happen when code runs
	• Run and test code

New key terms	**predict** – use information you have now to say what is going to happen in the future

You will need	• Bee-Bots or similar directional floor robots	**Key pedagogy**	Physical computing
	• A piece of paper to act as a starting mat for the Bee-Bot		

Activity	Instructions	Guidance
1	• Show learners a Bee-Bot and ask them to complete (📖✎ Page 24) Task A, 'Label the buttons'.	• Remind learners that they used Bee-Bots in the previous lesson. Explain that they will be using Bee-Bots again today. • Some learners may not have used the 'pause the code' button and will need help labelling this.
2	• Introduce learners to the definition of predict (📖 Page 32). • Tell learners that the Bee-Bot moves 15 cm each time it runs the forwards button code. They can use this information to predict the code needed to reach an object. • Split learners into small groups, each with a Bee-Bot. Place an object on the floor directly in front of each Bee-Bot and a paper 'starting mat' on the floor underneath each Bee-Bot. • Ask learners to complete the first question in (📖✎ Page 24) Task B, 'Predict the code: forwards'. • Use Discuss 9 (📖 Page 328).	• Learners should predict how many forward button presses are required to reach the object and stop at it. • Learners may use different techniques to predict the number of steps needed. Some could base it on sight alone, others might use the Bee-Bot to guess (the Bee-Bot is approximately 13 cm in length) and some might find or measure an object that is 15 cm in length. • It is important that learners place the Bee-Bot on the starting mat each time and that the starting mat does not move. Floor-friendly tape can be used to hold the mat in place.

Activity	Instructions	Guidance
3	• Ask learners to enter their code into the Bee-Bot so they can observe the results of their prediction. • Learners should clear the code and repeat the task until the Bee-Bot reaches the object. • Ask learners to complete the second question in (📖✏ Page 24) Task B, 'Predict the code: forwards'.	• Remind learners that they need to use the 'go' button to run the code they have entered and to use the 'clear the code' button between each attempt.
4	• Talk through the 'predict more code' section (📖 Page 33). • Move the objects so that they are still in front of the Bee-Bot starting mats but are now also off to one side. • Ask learners to complete (📖✏ Page 25) Task C, 'Predict the code: more than one direction'. • Use Discuss 10 (📖 Page 33).	• Learners should use the grids in the Workbook to create a plan. • Remind learners to reset their code after each attempt. • Some learners may choose to turn first. If so, they will need to turn twice in their code.
5	• Ask learners to complete (📖✏ Page 25) Task D, 'Reflect'. • Learners will reflect on their prediction skills.	• Get learners to think about whether they used the information that a Bee-Bot moves 15 cm each step, a Bee-Bot does a quarter turn, and a Bee-Bot doesn't move when it turns, to help them when predicting.

Build on this: Ask learners to draw and cut out a 15 cm ruler and use it to measure when making predictions. Discuss the advantages of using all the information you have in the best possible way when making predictions.

Chapter 3:	Lesson 4 Create a story		
Learning Objective	• Create a sequence to navigate a story		
You will need	• Bee-Bots or similar directional floor robots • Objects or printed photographs to create stories	**Key pedagogy**	Physical computing

Activity	Instructions	Guidance
1	• Tell learners they will be starting their project in this lesson. • Talk through the example (📖 Page 34), showing that the objects are photographs and printed material. • Talk through the captions and images from the cartoon strip (📖 Page 35) to tell the story. • Talk through the cartoon again. This time, draw attention to the code used to navigate the story.	• Tell learners that you have prepared some objects for them to use. Objects could be items from the classroom, printed photographs or used postcards from around the world. • If learners are covering a specific topic in another subject, you could use objects or images related to that topic.
2	• Split learners into groups. • Ask learners to complete (📖 Page 26) Task A, 'Plan your story'. • Learners will plan the objects for their story and the narrative of the story.	• Remind learners of the objects they can use. • Learners will be revisiting their plans in the next lesson, so ask learners to label their drawings. • The stories do not need directional writing. The important thing is the order their Bee-Bot will visit the objects and any details such as pauses. • Support learners as they are drawing and writing their stories. Make sure they are using all three drawn objects in their stories and that they have a clear order.
Build on this: Learners could check another learner's story to make sure the three objects have been used in the story.		

Chapter 3:	Lesson 5 Build and test your story		
Learning Objectives	• Write code to navigate a story • Run and test code that navigates a story		
You will need	• Bee-Bots or similar directional floor robots • Objects or printed photographs to create stories • A piece of paper to act as a starting mat for the Bee-Bot • The stories from Lesson 4 in the Workbook	**Key pedagogy**	Physical computing

Activity	Instructions	Guidance
1	• Talk through the example images (📖 Page 36) to show learners how the objects have been placed. • Split learners into the same groups as in the previous lesson. • Guide learners through gathering and placing their objects in their floor story area. They will need to refer to (📖 Page 26) Task A, 'Plan your story' from the previous lesson to see their chosen objects.	• Observe learners creating their story areas. • Remind learners that the Bee-Bot moves 15 cm and turns one quarter turn. The objects can therefore be spread out but not so far apart that it would mean entering very large amounts of code.
2	• Give out the Bee-Bots and tell groups to place their Bee-Bot on the starting mat. • Ask learners to complete (📖 Page 27) Task A, 'Code for your first object'. • Learners will write the predicted and actual code for the Bee-Bot to reach the first object in the story. • Use Discuss 11 (📖 Page 36).	• Learners could use pencils to draw their simple arrow routes so that they can rub them out as they test and edit them. Or they could create a series of improved routes underneath each other until they have a route that reaches the object. • Remind learners to use the 'clear the code' button between tests. • Some learners will struggle with left and right turns. Encourage them to move their Workbook to match the direction that the Bee-Bot is facing.

Activity	Instructions	Guidance
3	• Tell learners that they will now be creating the route from the first object to the second object. • Learners should place the Bee-Bot on the starting mat and run the code to reach the first object. When the code finishes learners should press the 'clear the code' button, but should keep the Bee-Bot in that position and direction. • Ask learners to complete (📖 Page 28) Task B, 'Code for your second object'. • Learners will write the predicted and actual code for the Bee-Bot to reach the second object in the story.	• You could give learners a second piece of paper to put under their Bee-Bot to mark the starting position for the second part of their route. • When learners have finished the Workbook task they could enter the code from the first and second routes to see them both working together. This may result in an additional small edit to make the routes perform perfectly together.
4	• Tell learners that they will now be creating the route from the second object to the third object. • Learners should place the Bee-Bot on the starting mat and run all the code created so far. When the code finishes learners should press the 'clear the code' button, but should keep the Bee-Bot in that position and direction. • Ask learners to complete (📖 Page 29) Task C, 'Code for your third object'. • Learners will write the predicted and actual code for the Bee-Bot to reach the third object in the story. • Use Discuss 12 (📖 Page 36).	• When learners have finished the Workbook task they should enter the code for the full story and make any edits needed to their final code.

Build on this: You could record the groups using the Bee-Bot to tell the story and play them back during the showcase in the next lesson.

Chapter 3:	Lesson 6 Showcase your story		
Learning Objective	• Showcase code that navigates a story		
You will need	• The stories from Lesson 4 in the Workbook • The code from Lesson 5 in the Workbook	**Key pedagogy**	Showcase

Activity	Instructions	Guidance
1	• Tell learners that they are going to share their stories. Read through the tips for storytelling (📖 Page 37). • Split learners into their groups and give them time to practise telling their stories.	• Encourage learners to each have a line as part of the storytelling. • If a learner doesn't want to speak, they could hold up the objects for the others.
2	• Conduct the showcase.	• If you have recorded learners using the Bee-Bot in the previous lesson, you could play the videos rather than have learners tell the story. • You could split learners into a few groups for the showcase rather than running as a whole-class activity. • Make sure learners talk through the story and the code they created.
3	• Ask learners to complete (📖 Page 30) Task A, 'Reflection'. • Learners should answer the two reflection questions by colouring in the stars. Guide learners with the task by explaining that colouring five stars is positive and one star is weak. • Celebrate your learners' achievements in creating code for a story. • Use the Reflection question (📖 Page 38).	• Celebrate how much work has gone into creating and showcasing their Bee-Bot stories.

Build on this: Give learners time to ask each other questions about their choice and positioning of objects and how they predicted, tested and wrote their final code.

Chapter 4 – How computers work

Project: Make a counting app to help with counting from 1 to 5

Chapter overview

In this chapter, learners will discover different types of input and output devices. They will then design an app in Scratch where they choose costumes for each number and record themselves saying each number from 1 to 5. They will learn how their app uses the inputs and outputs on a computer.

Chapter 4: Lesson summary		
Lesson	**Learning Objectives**	**Summary**
1	• State the components of computing systems, including; computer, keyboard, mouse, monitor, screen, touchpad, headphones, speaker, camera and microphone • Describe ways to input information into computers • Describe ways that information is output from computers	Learners identify the components of a computer or computing system. They learn that we use inputs to get information into a computer and outputs to get information out of a computer. They learn which computer components are inputs and which are outputs.
2	• Investigate inputs and outputs in an app	Learners investigate a pre-created Scratch app. They click or tap using inputs (mouse, touchpad or touchscreen) and observe graphics and sound effects using outputs (screen and speakers).
3	• Record sounds as input • Play sounds as output	Learners record sounds in a pre-recorded Scratch app. They use the Scratch Sound Editor to record their voices (using the computer microphone as input) and play the sounds back (using the computer speakers as output).
4	• Select costumes for sprites	Learners choose the costumes for the sprites in their Scratch app from a selection of diverse character sprites. They use their counting app. They hear their voices and see the costumes they chose.
5	• Record sounds for an app	Learners start working on a counting app project in Scratch. The code is provided for the app. Learners record their voices saying the numbers 1 to 5 into a pre-created Scratch app. They experiment with sound effects, including loudness, and choose the effects they prefer.
6	• Showcase counting apps	Learners showcase their counting apps to the class.

End of chapter project	Make a counting app to help with counting from 1 to 5
Example ideas that learners could design:	

Chapter 4 – How computers work

Project: Make a counting app to help with counting from 1 to 5

Name	

	Working towards (1)	Meets expected (2)	Exceeding expected (3)	Score
Sketches	• Chooses a costume in the workbook but needs assistance in Scratch	• Chooses a costume and selects it in Scratch; explains their choice	• Chooses a costume and selects it in Scratch. Explains their choice and demonstrates awareness of other sprites and costumes in Scratch.	
Final design	• Records sounds with assistance	• Follows instructions to record sounds	• Could explain to someone else how to record a sound in Scratch	
Everyday task	• Demonstrates the app in use but is unable to describe what it does	• Demonstrates and explains their app with some correct use of technical vocabulary	• Clearly demonstrates their app with considerable correct use of technical vocabulary: costume, sprite, input, output, click/tap	

Teacher feedback	
Learner response	

Chapter 4:	Lesson 1 Parts of a computer
Learning Objectives	• State the components of computing systems, including; computer, keyboard, mouse, monitor, screen, touchpad, headphones, speaker, camera and microphone • Describe ways to input data into computers • Describe ways that information is output from computers
New key terms	**computer system** – computer with its connected parts **component** – part of a computer system **mouse** – component that you move to point to things on a computer screen **keyboard** – component that you use to type letters and numbers on a computer **screen (or monitor)** – component that shows pictures and videos from a computer **printer** – component that can put pictures and words on paper **speakers** – component that can play sound from a computer **touchpad (or trackpad)** – part of a laptop computer that you use to point to things on a computer screen by moving your finger **touchscreen** – component that shows pictures and videos and allows you to point to things with your finger **headphones** – component that can play sound from a computer **microphone** – component that can get sound into a computer **webcam** – component that can get pictures and video into a computer **input** – component that allows a person to enter information into a computer **output** – component that presents information to a person

You will need	• **Optional:** Computer components such as a keyboard and mouse	**Key pedagogy**	Classroom talk

Activity	Instructions	Guidance
1	• Introduce the definitions of computer system and component (📖 Page 40). • Use Discuss 1 (📖 Page 41).	• If you have computers in the room, ask learners to point to components. • Explain that some computers have components that are separate but connected (e.g. a computer with a separate screen/monitor) and some computers have different components built into them (for example, a laptop includes a screen and doesn't have a separate monitor).

Activity	Instructions	Guidance
2	• Explain the difference between inputs and outputs, using the definitions on (📖 Page 41). • Talk through the example using the picture. • Ask learners to complete (📖✏ Pages 31 and 32) Tasks A, 'Find the inputs' and B, 'Find the outputs'. 　• Learners circle images of inputs and outputs.	• Learners will be introduced to the word 'data' in Chapter 6. In this chapter, the word 'information' is used to describe what is going in and out of the computer. • If you have some sample equipment to demonstrate to your learners, you can show these as well here. • Provide answers straight away to help address misconceptions quickly.
3	• Recap the terms 'input', 'output' and 'computer system' (📖 Page 41). • Ask for examples of inputs. • Ask for examples of outputs. • Explain that computers wouldn't be very useful to people if they didn't have inputs and outputs. • Use Discuss 2 (📖 Page 41).	• Highlight that some devices, such as the touchscreen on a tablet, can be an input and an output.

Build on this: Can learners think of any input or output components that have not been mentioned in the lesson?

Chapter 4:	Lesson 2 Inputs and outputs in an app		
Learning Objective	• Investigate inputs and outputs in an app		
You will need	• Computers or tablets set up to run Scratch. Check that they can play sound. • The Scratch starter project (Website C4L2R1)	**Key pedagogy**	Develop practical skills

Activity	Instructions	Guidance
1	• Use Discuss 3 (📖 Page 42). • Go through the recap of inputs in the Student's Book. • Use Discuss 4 (📖 Page 42). • Go through the recap of outputs in the Student's Book.	• Examples of inputs: mouse, microphone, touchscreen, trackpad, keyboard, webcam. • Examples of outputs: screen, speakers, headphones, printer.

2	• Tell learners that they are going to investigate a Scratch app (📖 Page 43). • Demonstrate opening the Scratch project (Website C4L2R1) • Demonstrate clicking or tapping on the chick to hear a chirping sound. • Ask learners to complete (📖✏️ Pages 33 and 34) Tasks A, 'Investigate a Scratch app', B, 'Which of these inputs did you use?' and C, 'Which of these outputs did you use?'. • Learners investigate the Scratch project.	• Check that learners are able to play sound from their device. They should be able to tap/click on an input and hear the output through the speakers. If you are having difficulties, see the Scratch guidance at the start of this Teacher's Guide for troubleshooting advice.
3	• Demonstrate clicking on each sprite in the app. Ask learners for their answer and then give the correct answer. • Discuss 5 (📖 Page 43). • Demonstrate the location of the microphone and speaker(s) on the computers that you use in school.	• The input depends on the devices you are using: mouse, trackpad or touchscreen. Optionally, you may have used a keyboard for number keys. • The outputs used are screen (or monitor) and speakers or headphones. • If using laptops, tablets or monitors with speakers, explain that they have speakers inside them.

Build on this: **The Scratch project has been set up to use keys as inputs, as well as clicking or tapping. You can use these as an extension. The keys are 1, 2, 3, 4, 5, 6. You will need a computer with a physical keyboard connected.**

Chapter 4:	Lesson 3 Sound input and output		
Learning Objectives	• Record sounds as input • Play sounds as output		
You will need	• Computers or tablets set up to run Scratch. Check that they can play sound and record sound in Scratch before the lesson. • The Scratch starter project (Website C4L3R1)	**Key pedagogy**	Develop practical skills

Activity	Instructions	Guidance
1	• Remind learners about Scratch and the app that had been created for them in the previous lesson (📖 Pages 42 and 43). • Let them know that during this lesson they will use Scratch to record their own sounds (📖 Page 44). • Use Discuss 6 (📖 Page 44).	• This is a practice lesson to get learners familiar with recording sound in Scratch. They are not working on their app yet. • The answer to the discussion question is an input. They will use a microphone to input their own sounds into a Scratch program.
2	• Demonstrate, on your teacher computer, how to open the Scratch project (<u>Website C4L3R1</u>) • Demonstrate how to record a sound, using the step-by-step instructions (📖 Page 45). • If you are using a mouse or trackpad, demonstrate accidentally clicking on 'Choose a sound' instead of hovering. Demonstrate clicking 'Back' to try again. • Give learners time to record their first sound.	• If you are using desktop or laptop computers with a trackpad or mouse, you need to hover (move the mouse pointer) over the 'Add sound' button. If you accidentally tap it, you will go into the 'Choose a sound' window and will need to click 'Back' and try again. • If you are using the microphone in Scratch for the first time, you will need to click 'Allow'.
3	• Demonstrate how to apply different effects to the sounds: Faster, Slower, Louder, Softer (📖 Page 46). • Demonstrate 'Undo'. • Ask learners to complete (📖 Page 35) Task A, 'Try sound effects'. • Learners will answer questions about the sound effects they try.	• Encourage learners to try different effects. They can easily undo any effects they don't want to keep.
4	• Use Discuss 7 (📖 Page 46).	• Effects include: Faster, Slower, Louder, Softer, Reverse, Robot.
5	• Demonstrate recording another sound. Recap recording sounds. • Demonstrate switching between sounds in the Sound Editor, using the guidance in Student's Book (📖 Page 46). • Give learners the opportunity to record more sounds and explore effects. • Ask learners to complete (📖 Page 36) Task B, 'Match the pictures'. Learners match up sound effects to their icon in Scratch.	• If your learners are sharing computers, make sure everyone gets a chance to record their voice. • This project is just for practice so it is not important to save projects. However, you can use this as another opportunity to practise saving.
6	• Use Discuss 8 (📖 Page 46).	• Choose learners to play the sounds they recorded.

Activity	Instructions	Guidance

Build on this: **Learners could role-play the different sound effects.**

Chapter 4:	Lesson 4 Choose costumes for your app		
Learning Objective	• Select costumes for sprites		
You will need	• Computers or tablets set up to run Scratch	**Key pedagogy**	Develop practical skills

Activity	Instructions	Guidance
1	• Introduce the project brief (📖 Page 47). • Demonstrate a finished project (for example, (<u>Website C4L4R1</u>) • Use Discuss 9 (📖 Page 47).	• Explain that you will be making an app to help children to learn to count from 1 to 5. • The project will use the microphone and mouse/trackpad/touchscreen as an input and the screen and speakers as outputs.
2	• Recap Scratch terminology and set-up, including sprites, costumes and the stage (📖 Page 47).	• Refer to Scratch on your teacher computer screen as you recap the terms. • In this lesson, learners will need to click on sprites under the stage to select a sprite to record sound. They will also need to click on sprites on the stage to play the sounds. Make sure they know the difference.
3	• Explain that in this lesson learners will be choosing the costumes for their sprites. • Ask learners to complete (📖 Page 37) Task A, 'Choose costumes for your app'.	• Make sure learners understand that they need to circle one costume from each *column* in the Workbook.
4	• Demonstrate how learners will open the Scratch project on their computers (<u>Website C4L4R2</u>). • Demonstrate selecting the costume for the first sprite, using the guidance (📖 Page 47).	

Activity	Instructions	Guidance
5	• Demonstrate how learners will save their apps.	• Show how to do this on the computers or tablets and the version of Scratch that you are using. • You could ask a learner to demonstrate this to the class if you think they are able to at this point. • Learners will be adding to their projects in the next lesson so it is very important that they are saved.
6	• Use Discuss 10 (📖 Page 47). • Explain that in the next lesson you will be recording voices so that the sprites can say their numbers.	• Did learners choose costumes that look like their friends or family?

Build on this: Learners could work with a partner to check that their choices in the Workbook match the costumes in their app.

Chapter 4:	Lesson 5 Record sounds for your app		
Learning Objective	• Record sounds for an app		
You will need	• Computers or tablets set up to run Scratch	**Key pedagogy**	Develop practical skills

Activity	Instructions	Guidance
1	• Explain that in this lesson learners will be recording their voices saying the numbers from 1 to 5 (📖 Page 48).	• Optionally, you can allow learners to invite other learners to record voices for their app. Let your learners know if they are allowed to do this.
2	• Demonstrate opening the Scratch projects from the previous lesson. • Demonstrate clicking on the number 1 sprite and recording yourself saying 'one'. Use the step-by-step guidance (📖 Page 48). • Tell learners to follow the instructions to record the sound for Sprite 1.	• Show how to do this on the computers or tablets and version of Scratch that you are using.

Activity	Instructions	Guidance
3	• Demonstrate clicking on the number 2 sprite and recording yourself saying 'two'. • Explain that each sound belongs to a sprite. It's **really important** to click on the correct sprite before you record. • Tell learners to follow the instructions to record the sounds for Sprites 2 to 5. They should then mark the sprites off, using (📖✏ Page 38) Task A, 'Record sounds one to five'.	• The project has code to play 'recording1' when clicked. Learners do not need to use this code and must not delete it. If they accidentally delete the code, you can copy the code from another sprite for them. • Expect some learners to forget to select the correct sprite before recording. Delete the sound and tell them to select the correct sprite and re-record the sound.
4	• Ask 'Where do you click before recording a sound for a sprite?' • Ask learners to complete (📖✏ Page 39) Task B, 'Where should you click?'. • Learners will answer questions about interacting with the Scratch program.	• Explain that we often make mistakes when we are learning, but we can fix them.
5	• Demonstrate how to **save** projects again.	• It's **very important** that projects are saved as learners will need them for the showcase in the next lesson.
6	• Use Discuss 11 (📖 Page 44). • Explain that learners will be showcasing their counting apps in the next lesson.	• Encourage learners to think about what kind of voices a young child would like to hear. It's important to consider who you are making an app for.

Build on this: **Learners could add sound effects to the sound for each sprite.**

Chapter 4:	Lesson 6 Showcase your counting app		
Learning Objective	• Showcase counting apps		
You will need	• The saved Scratch counting apps that learners have created	**Key pedagogy**	Showcase

Activity	Instructions	Guidance
1	• Explain that learners will be showcasing their counting apps. • Run through the tips for showcasing (📖 Page 49).	• If you have time, you could encourage learners to practise with a partner.
2	• Complete the showcase activity (📖 Page 49).	• You could split the class into groups to showcase to each other.
3	• Ask learners to complete the (📖 Page 40) Task A, 'Reflection'. Guide learners with the task by explaining that five stars is positive and one star is weak.	• Focus on the importance of making an app for children to use.
4	• Reflection: 'How does it feel to have made your own app?' (📖 Page 50). • Celebrate how much work has gone into creating and showcasing their apps.	• You may wish to keep learners' projects in a specific place (online or offline) to keep as a portfolio of their work across the stage. • If you have younger children in the school, you could invite them to try the apps.

Build on this: **Learners could play with each other's apps and discuss them.**

Chapter 5 – Create with code 2

Project: Create a scene with layers to show a view from a window

Chapter overview

In this chapter, learners will learn about the importance of ordering instructions to complete a task. They will do this through an unplugged activity before trying it out in real code with Scratch. They will then design a layered view from a window using the Scratch platform.

Chapter 5: Lesson summary		
Lesson	Learning Objectives	Summary
1	• Describe the importance of the order of instructions in an algorithm • List ordered instructions to complete everyday tasks	Learners explore the correct order for instructions to build a 'real-world' stacking tower. They apply that thinking to a digital version in a Scratch program.
2	• State that programs can contain errors • Define the term 'debugging' • Identify errors in programs	Learners find the errors in everyday situations and discuss them with the class. They debug the code that was designed to create an animation.
3	• List the correct order for a sequence	Learners work with a real-world piece of art that must be built in the correct order. They create their own woodland scenes, using layered images on paper.
4	• Design an app that creates a scene	Learners are introduced to their project brief, which is to create a layered scene in Scratch showing a view from a window. They choose the window, animal, tree and background for their designs.
5	• Build and test an app that creates a scene	Learners build their apps in Scratch, based on their choices. They place the code blocks in the correct order to build their designed scene. They also complete some testing to make sure that their order is correct.
6	• Showcase an app that creates a scene	Learners showcase their work to their peers and reflect on their progress in this chapter.

End of chapter project	Create a layered scene to show a view from a window
Example ideas that learners could design:	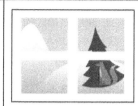  

Chapter 5 – Create with Code 2

Project: Create a scene with layers to show a view from a window

Name	

	Working towards (1)	Meets expected (2)	Exceeding expected (3)	Score
Sketches	• Some design choices were made about the costumes for the layered scene	• All design choices were made about the costumes for the layered scene	• All design choices were made about the costumes for the layered scene. The learner could explain why they knew their layers were ordered correctly in their design	
Final design	• Some of the code blocks were placed in the correct order	• All of the code blocks were placed in the correct order	• All of the code blocks were placed in the correct order. The learner could explain how they knew their code blocks were in the correct order.	
Everyday task	• Some tests had been carried out	• All tests had been carried out	• All tests had been carried out and debugging had taken place to ensure the app worked correctly	

Teacher feedback	
Learner response	

Chapter 5:	Lesson 1 Stacking tower			
Learning Objectives	• Describe the importance of the order of instructions in an algorithm • List ordered instructions to complete everyday tasks			
New key terms	**code block** – single line of code in Scratch			
You will need	• Either a stacking rings toy or a paper-based version using different sized cut-out circles. • Scratch installed on your computers or access to the Scratch website • The 'Stacking tower' Scratch program (Website C5L1R1)		**Key pedagogy**	Real-world contexts

Activity	Instructions	Guidance
1	• Remind learners that it is important to write instructions, and algorithms, in the correct order. • Show learners the comic strip (📖 Page 52) and use Discuss 1. • Have a short discussion until learners have worked out the correct order.	• Remind learners that 'algorithm' was a new key term in Chapter 3. • You could ask learners to test out their shoes and socks algorithm if there is time.
2	• Show learners the stacking rings toy (📖 Page 52) and the real version that you have prepared for the lesson. • Ask learners to give you the first instruction for placing the rings in the correct order. • Select learners or invite 'hands up' to ask for each instruction until the tower is complete. • Did they get it right the first time? What were the exact instructions?	• You may wish to repeat this activity a few times, asking for instructions from different learners if needed.
3	• Ask learners to complete (📖 Page 41) Task A, 'Stack the rings'. Learners write the correct order for the stacking rings picture.	• Learners who need extra support could use your physical demonstration toy to troubleshoot.
4	• Ask learners what their answers were to the Workbook activity and check that they understand the correct order.	• They could discuss in pairs and change their answers before discussing with the class.

Activity	Instructions	Guidance
5	• Show learners the stacking tower project in the Scratch example (📖 Page 53). • Use Discuss 2 (📖 Page 53).	• You could break this question down more by asking, 'Which block do you think should go first?'
6	• Demonstrate how to open the Stacking Tower Scratch program to your learners (<u>Website C5L1R1</u>). • Show learners how to detach blocks and reattach them in a different order. Focus first on the skill of attaching and reattaching blocks to build the digital skills required for the computational thinking part of this task.	• Read the guidance at the beginning of the Teacher's Guide for a reminder of how to use Scratch in your setting. • Note that you can zoom in on the code blocks to make them easier to click/tap and drag.
7	• Ask learners to complete (📖 Page 42) Task B, 'The correct order'. Learners are given instructions to keep adjusting their blocks in Scratch until they have found the correct order. When they have found the correct order, they should draw it in their Workbooks.	• This is an important activity for building resilience and self-efficacy. Learners will not only be using 'drag and drop', but also their computational thinking skills to predict and problem solve. • Be careful that this activity doesn't become a competition for who finishes first. Give learners time to explore and discover and let them know that it is completely normal to get it wrong a few times before they get it right.
8	• Use the Reflection question (📖 Page 53).	• This is another key moment to reinforce that the activity isn't a competition and everyone is developing their problem-solving skills. This is what should be celebrated – not who did it fastest.

Build on this: Learners could discuss in pairs or as a class how the Scratch activity was similar to the real-world activity used at the beginning of the lesson. Are there any other toys that they use in the 'real world' that could become games in the digital world?

Chapter 5:	Lesson 2 Debugging		
Learning Objectives	• State that programs can contain errors • Define the term 'debugging' • Identify errors in programs		
New key terms	debugging – finding errors in code and fixing them		
You will need	• Computers with Scratch installed or access to the Scratch website • The Sand Bucket Scratch project (Website C5L2R1) • The Sand Bucket Fixed (Website C5L2R2)	Key pedagogy	Real-world contexts Parson's problems

Activity	Instructions	Guidance
1	• Introduce the definition of debugging and show learners the three images (📖 Page 54). Use Discuss 3.	• Learners could discuss in pairs or you could lead a class discussion on the images. • The first image needs the umbrella to be open. • The second image should say the answer is 2. • The third image should show the buttons done up in the correct order.
2	• Introduce the sand bucket Scratch project to your learners (📖 Page 55). • The program has been created by a child to produce an animation that will show a sand bucket filling up. The screenshot in the book shows the first error. The white layer of sand appears first. • Instruct your learners to open the Scratch project themselves. They should run the project to see the error happening in the animation.	• You may wish to run the project to the whole class first and discuss the error, or you can choose to allow learners to investigate it themselves. • They should run it several times to try to spot the errors.
3	• Ask learners to complete (📖 Page 43) Task A, 'Find the error' and circle the error.	• Ask learners where they circled. They might have circled just the 'White' block or all of them. This is OK at this stage.

4	• Direct learners to now fix the error that they have spotted in the Scratch project by moving the blocks around. This is a very similar skill to the one used in the previous lesson. • They should test their code to make sure it works. If it doesn't, they can try again.	• You may need to remind learners how to drag apart the blocks and reattach them.
5	• Once they have fixed the error ask learners to complete (📖 Page 43) Task B, 'Fix the error' in which they draw the fixed program.	• You may wish to share the fixed program with your learners. • The correct order for the code blocks follows this sequence: 'Brown', 'Orange', 'Yellow', 'White'.
6	• Ask the Reflection question (📖 Page 55).	• Encourage use of the term 'debugging' to explain that they will find the error and fix it. • Remind learners that debugging is a normal part of coding and even the best programmers in the world have errors in their code.

Build on this: Learners could create a new error in the code and ask a partner to debug it.

Chapter 5:	Lesson 3 Layered scene		
Learning Objective	• List the correct order for a sequence		
New key terms	**layers** – placing objects on top of each other, for example a cake could have three layers of sponge		
You will need	• A copy of the 'Layered scene' worksheets for each learner or pair. You may want to cut out the worksheet to create a class set if your learners need a lot of support with using scissors. • Glue • Scissors • Coloured pencils	**Key pedagogy**	Get creative!

Activity	Instructions	Guidance
1	• Ask 'Look out of the window. What is the furthest thing away that you can see?' (📖 Page 56). • Use Discuss 4 (📖 Page 56).	• These questions should be adjusted for your setting. If you do not have windows with a view from your classroom, ask learners to stand at one end of the classroom or a hall and spot the object that is furthest away and the object that is closest.
2	• Use the jungle scene example (📖 Page 56) to show learners what a layer is and why it is important to place layers in the correct order to get the correct outcome.	• If you have a pop-up book that uses similar layering, you could use it to demonstrate to learners. This would link nicely with a language lesson for cross-curricular study.
3	• Show the example images that use layering (📖 Page 57). • Use Discuss 5 (📖 Page 57).	• If you have a real-life layered scene that you could use as an example, it would be good to display this now.
4	• Ask learners to complete (📖✐ Page 45) Task A, 'Order the layers'. Learners order the layers of a scene. Layer 1 is the background layer, moving up to layer 4, which is the front layer.	• You could prepare a finished version of the layered scene activity for learners to physically move around to help them determine the order of the layers.

5	• Distribute materials for learners to create their own layered scene. You should use the 'Layered scene' worksheet (see pages 80 and 81) for this.
	• Instruct learners to cut out the shapes if this has not been prepared.
	• Instruct learners to colour their scenes and to be as imaginative as they like.
	• Instruct learners to place their layers in the correct order. They can glue them together if this is appropriate for your class.
		• The purpose of this lesson is to give learners another tangible experience in creating the correct order for a sequence. Alternative creative ways to do this are to:
		  • use 'sticky-felt' craft kits to create layers for a scene
		  • use pre-cut simple shapes such as circles, triangles, squares and rectangles to build a face or an animal
		  • build layered scenes using plastic building bricks.

6	• If there is time, give learners an opportunity to have a mini showcase with a partner to show their designs to each other.	• You could also use this time to reinforce the importance of having the correct order.

Build on this: Learners could add an extra layer to the scene using their own hand-drawn designs.

Chapter 5:	Lesson 4 Design your scene		
Learning Objective	• Design an app that creates a scene		
You will need	• 'Create a scene' Scratch example project (<u>Website C5L4R1</u>)	**Key pedagogy**	Get creative

Activity	Instructions	Guidance
1	• Remind learners of the project brief, which is to create a layered scene to show a view from a window (📖 Page 58). • Explain that they will choose from a variety of animals, window frames, trees and backgrounds in Scratch to build their own scenes.	• Relate this back to the physical layered scenes that they created in the previous lesson.
2	• Open the 'Create a scene' Scratch project on your teacher computer (<u>Website C5L4R1</u>). Show learners the type of app that they will be creating. • Press the green flag and show learners that the scene is built from the background to the window frame. • Use Discuss 6 (📖 Page 58). Remind them of how important it is to get the instructions in the correct order.	• Again, use the real-life example that they created in the previous lesson to relate the concept of layering and order.
3	• Ask learners to complete (📖✏ Pages 46 and 47), 'Choose your costumes'. Learners choose costumes for each of the sprites.	• Specify that they should only choose one object from each category.
4	• Ask learners to complete (📖✏ Page 47) Task B, 'Order your sprites'. Learners write the correct order of the sprites for their layered scene.	• Remind learners of the activities from the previous lesson to help support them with this activity.
5	• Give learners some time to share their choices with a partner. • Direct learners to reflect on the costumes that they have chosen and the order of their sprites (📖 Page 58). Use the Reflect question (📖 Page 58).	• The correct order for the sprites is: Background, Trees, Animal, Window Frame. Make sure that learners have understood this correctly. • Show the project again in Scratch to help if needed.

Build on this: You could ask learners what they would add to the scene to improve it. They can be as imaginative as they like!

Chapter 5:	Lesson 5 Build and test scenes		
Learning Objective	• Build and test an app that creates a scene		
You will need	• Scratch installed on all learner computers • 'Create a scene starter' Scratch starter project (Website C5L5R1)	**Key pedagogy**	Get creative

Activity	Instructions	Guidance
1	• Remind learners of the choices they made in the previous lesson for their 'Create a scene' apps. • Demonstrate how to open the Scratch starter project to learners (Website C5L5R1). • Remind them of how to select sprites and choose a costume for a sprite.	• This is the third time during this Stage that learners have clicked on a sprite and chosen a costume for that sprite. They should, therefore, be familiar with the steps, but use questioning to check how much they remember.
2	• Direct learners to find their sprite and costume choices (📖 Pages 47 and 48). • Direct learners to select them in the Scratch starter project.	• If learners don't like their choices, they can choose new ones at this stage.
3	• Learners must now order the code blocks so they display in the correct order when they click the green flag. • Ask learners to plan the order of their code blocks (📖 Page 48), 'Order the code blocks'.	• If learners need more support with this, you could open and project the starter project from your teacher computer and troubleshoot issues. For example, connecting the code blocks in different orders then running the code will very visually show on the Stage the results of mis-ordering the layers.
4	• Once they have decided on their chosen order direct learners to try it out in the Scratch starter project. See the step-by-step instructions (📖 Page 60). • Demonstrate how to find the Code sprite and drag blocks together. Also, remind learners how to attach and detach blocks in case they make a mistake.	• Use the zoom tool if learners are struggling with selecting the blocks that they need.

Activity	Instructions	Guidance
5	• Direct learners to (📖✏ Page 49) Task B, 'Test'. Learners should mark next to the 'I can' statements if they can see each sprite. If they cannot see a particular sprite, they should adjust their code until they get it right. • Remember to ask learners to **save** their work using the method that you have chosen for your setting. • Use Discuss 7 (📖 Page 60).	• Support with reading by reading the 'I can' statements aloud to the class.
6	• Use the Reflect question (📖 Page 60).	• Remind learners that it is normal for code to not work as expected the first few times that you run it. Debugging is an important part of learning to code.

Build on this: Learners could change their backgrounds, trees, animals and windows to see if they prefer another combination of costumes.

Chapter 5:	Lesson 6 Showcase your scene		
Learning Objective	• Showcase an app that creates a scene		
You will need	• The Scratch projects from the previous lesson	**Key pedagogy**	Showcase

Activity	Instructions	Guidance
1	• Demonstrate how to open the Scratch projects from the previous lesson.	• See the teacher guidance at the beginning of this Teacher's Guide for support with this.
2	• Remind learners what a showcase is (📖 Page 61) and give them time to practise what they want to say.	• Observe learners practising and remind them to speak loudly and clearly. • Encourage them to include details about their choices, debugging activity and feelings about their project.
3	• Showcase the learner projects.	• Use the showcase section at the beginning of this Teacher's Guide to decide how best to run the session.

Activity	Instructions	Guidance
4	• Ask your learners to reflect on their projects by completing (📖 Page 50) Task A, 'Reflect'. They should answer the three reflection questions by colouring in the number of stars. Guide learners with the task by explaining that colouring five stars is positive and one star is weak.	
5	• Give learners some time to share their reflections with their peers (in pairs or small groups). • Use the Reflect question (📖 Page 62). • Celebrate learners' achievements!	• You could right-click on the Stage for each project to save a picture of each scene. You could then create a class display or presentation showing all the different combinations of scenes that have been made.
Build on this: **Learners could improve their apps based on feedback from their peers.**		

Chapter 6 – Connect the world

Project: Design a webpage on a topic of your choice

Chapter overview

In this chapter, learners will explore wired and wireless connections. They will also discover what a computer network is and that the internet is a big network of computers. They will then learn about the World Wide Web and how to use it safely. Finally, they will design their own webpages on a chosen topic.

Lesson	Learning Objectives	Summary
	Chapter 6: Lesson summary	
1	• State that computers and components can be wired or wireless	Learners discover that connections between computers and components can be wired or wireless. They participate in a role-play activity to communicate over a wired connection.
2	• Define a network • Explain that the internet connects computers all around the world • Describe scenarios where the internet may not be available	Learners explore the definition of a network and discover that the internet connects computers all around the world. They participate in a role-play activity to communicate using a network.
3	• Define the World Wide Web • Define a webpage • Recognise and report inappropriate digital content or activity	Learners discover that webpages are accessed from the World Wide Web (WWW). Learners role-play an activity for staying safe on the WWW.
4	• Plan a webpage	Learners choose a topic for their webpage and sketch a design. They identify the parts of a webpage.
5	• Design a webpage	Learners complete the detailed design for their webpages. They describe what makes a good website.
6	• Showcase the design of a webpage	Learners showcase their completed webpage designs to an audience.

End of chapter project	Design a webpage on a topic of your choice
Example ideas that learners could design:	

Chapter 6 – Connect the world

Project: Design a webpage on a topic of your choice

Name	

	Working towards (1)	Meets expected (2)	Exceeding expected (3)	Score
Sketches	• Partially planned a webpage; needed guidance	• Chose a topic and sketched a webpage with appropriate parts	• Chose a topic and sketched a detailed webpage with effective selection of a variety of parts	
Final design	• Partially designed a webpage; needed guidance	• Designed a webpage with appropriate content for their topic, layout and age group	• Designed a detailed webpage with appropriate content and effective use of a variety of parts	
Everyday task	• Partially demonstrated their webpage	• Demonstrated and described their webpage with some use of correct vocabulary	• Demonstrated and described their webpage with significant use of correct vocabulary such as heading, type of webpage (e.g. information or tutorial), pictures and buttons.	

Teacher feedback	
Learner response	

Chapter 6:	Lesson 1 Wired and wireless connections		
Learning Objective	• State that computers and components can be wired or wireless		
New key terms	**wired connection** – when devices communicate with each other through a wire **wireless connection** – when devices communicate with each other without a wire connecting the devices		
You will need	• Pre-prepared cup and string for wired communication: • 1 cup for each child in your class • a way to make holes in the cups • a 2-metre length of string for each pair of cups, threaded through the holes and knotted.	**Key pedagogy**	Unplugged

Activity	Instructions	Guidance
1	• Introduce the new chapter (📖 Page 63). • Explain that in this lesson learners will be finding out how computers and components communicate with each other (📖 Page 64). • Remind learners of the definition of a computer system. • Introduce the role-play activity (📖 Page 64). Put learners in pairs. Give them pre-prepared cups and strings and show them how to communicate with one partner talking and the other listening.	• Strings need to be pulled tight. • Remind learners that they don't need to shout; their voice will travel through the string.

Activity	Instructions	Guidance
2	• Explain that some computers and components communicate using a wired connection (📖 Page 65). • Use Discuss 1 (📖 Page 65). • Give learners time to complete (📖✐ Page 51) Task A, 'Connect the computer systems'. Discuss the answers. Did they add all the wires?	• Demonstrate wired connections in the classroom. This could be a wired computer mouse or a cable from the teacher computer to the projector. • For the discussion question, learners might say that the message could travel to them, but they might also say that they couldn't move too far from the other person. • Learners might be used to using a mouse or headphones that don't have wires. This is a good time to point out that some types of device can have both wired and wireless versions.
3	• Introduce wireless communication (📖 Page 65). • Explain that your voice travels through the air. When wireless devices communicate they also send information through the air. • Talk through the picture discussing the controllers. Highlight that one has a wire and one is wireless. • Use Discuss 2 (📖 Page 65).	• Demonstrate wireless connections in the classroom; for example, wireless keyboards, mice, headphones or wireless toys.
4	• Give learners time to complete (📖✐ Page 52) Task B, 'Find the wireless connections'. Discuss the answers.	• We sometimes talk about 'wireless devices' but a device might use wired and wireless communication for different purposes.

Activity	Instructions	Guidance
5	• Use Discuss 3 (📖 Page 65).	• Wired connections are often faster, but wireless connections can be more convenient. Learners might say that wireless connections can be useful when you need to move around (this is true for headphones and games controllers, for example). • Wireless devices can get lost. • This is an opportunity to remind learners that they need to be careful when using wired headphones, and to be careful not to lose a wireless games controller or mouse.

Build on this: Learners could have a discussion in pairs about the wired and wireless components they have used, and choose one component they thought was best suited to be wired and one that they preferred to use wirelessly.

Chapter 6	Lesson 2 Networks and the internet		
Learning Objectives	• Define a computer network • Explain that the internet connects computers all around the world • Describe scenarios where the internet may not be available		
New key terms	**computer network** – group of computers connected so that they can communicate **internet** – big network that connects computers and digital devices around the world		
You will need	• For each group of six children: • eight pieces of string varying from 30 cm to 100 cm in length (you can reuse the string from the cups activity in Lesson 1) • sheet of blank paper	**Key pedagogy**	Unplugged

Activity	Instructions	Guidance
1	• Discuss the definition of a computer network ([📖] Page 66). • Explain that your school computers are connected together in a network.	• Provide an example from your school. Is there a printer connected to your computer network? Does your school have a reception area or school library with a computer connected to the internet?
2	• Give learners time to complete ([📖] Page 53) Task A, 'Connect to the printer', where they draw wires to connect computers with a printer in a network. Discuss the answers.	• Check that learners understand that a computer just needs a connection to one other computer in the network to access the printer. • Note that individual computers usually connect to a router rather than directly to each other. This will be covered in Stage 5, 'Connect the World'.
3	• Introduce the role-play activity ([📖] Page 67). • Put learners into groups of six and give each group eight strings. Ask them to make a network. • Give a blank sheet of paper to one learner in each group and tell them that this is a message. Say who you want the message to reach. • Remind learners that they can only pass a message if there is a string. • Remove some strings from each group so that not all children are connected. • Repeat the activity. • Use Discuss 4 ([📖] Page 67).	• Act out one round of the activity with a group in front of the class to ensure everyone understands. • After giving out strings, pause and make sure that every child in the network is connected.
4	• Give learners time to complete ([📖] Page 54) Task B, 'Send a message' where they draw arrows to show how a message can get from one computer to another. • Make it clear that learners can only draw arrows on the lines. They cannot add new lines. • Discuss the answers. Explain that there is more than one correct path. As long as the computers are connected, the message will be able to reach Computer 2.	• Mention that it can be useful to have multiple connections, for example if one wire gets damaged.

5	• Discuss the definition of the internet ([📖] Page 67). • Make sure you explain that computers can use wired or wireless connections to connect to the internet.	• You could mention that computers in your school connect to the internet. • The internet is used for sending messages, downloading and updating apps, and accessing websites.

6	• Give learners time to complete ([📖✎] Page 54) Task C, 'Connecting to the internet'.
	• Use Discuss 5 ([📖] Page 67).
		• For the discussion, examples could include:
		  • no Wi-Fi password
		  • wire unplugged
		  • power cut
		  • no Wi-Fi (or no data).
		• Learners may have heard people say that they couldn't access the internet, or have 'no Wi-Fi'. Explain that this means that their computer cannot connect to the internet.

Build on this: Learners could draw a picture of a computer in your school that connects to the internet. They could discuss with a partner whether it uses wired or wireless communication to connect to the internet.

Chapter 6:	Lesson 3 Webpages and the World Wide Web		
Learning Objectives	• Define the World Wide Web • Define a webpage • Recognise and report inappropriate digital content or activity		
New key terms	**webpage** – document that your computer gets from the internet **website** – collection of webpages **World Wide Web (WWW)** – all the webpages on the internet		
You will need	• Blank sheets of paper to use as webpages for role play • **Optional:** Access to computers or tablets that can access the internet	**Key pedagogy**	Develop practical skills

Activity	Instructions	Guidance
1	• Remind learners that the internet connects computers around the world. • Introduce the definitions of webpage, website and the World Wide Web (WWW) (📖 Page 68). • Demonstrate visiting webpages on an age-appropriate website.	• Choose an age-appropriate website that is relevant to your learners, for example the National Geographic Kids website, 'Animals' tab.
2	• Give learners time to complete (📖 Page 55) Task A, 'Fill in the letters'. Learners complete sentences about the World Wide Web. • Discuss the answers.	• Can learners remember what WWW stands for? • Explain how amazing it is that you can access webpages from all around the world on your computer.

3	• Cover the material on staying safe on computers (📖 Page 69).
	• Introduce the role-play activity. Use blank sheets of paper as 'webpages' that the children look at.
	  • Get one of your learners to demonstrate what they would do before using a computer (ask a grown up). Then, give them the 'webpage'.
	  • Get one of your learners to demonstrate what they would do if they see something that worries them (tell a grown up).
	  • Ask groups to complete the role play, asking and telling a grown up.
		• Explain the kinds of worrying material children could find on the internet in a way that is appropriate for your learners. This could include content that is scary or too grown up.
		• Different children will find different content worrying. Explain that they should always tell a grown up, even if they are not sure there's a problem.
		• Tell your learners to look away from the computer if they find something worrying. Role-play this too.

4	• Give learners time to complete (📖 Page 55) Task B, 'Staying safe', where learners answer questions about staying safe on a computer. • Demonstrate how to visit a specific website.	• If you don't have easy access to computers or tablets that your learners can use, you can complete this activity as a class. • Example website: National Geographic Kids, 'Animals' tab

5	• Use Discuss 6 (📖 Page 69).
	• Remind learners that the WWW is amazing but it's very important to stay safe when using it.
		• This is an opportunity to recap:
		  • Ask a grown up before visiting a website.
		  • Tell a grown up if you see something that worries you.

Activity	Instructions	Guidance

Build on this: **Show learners how to visit a specific website and encourage them to discuss the different pictures and text they can see.**

Chapter 6:	Lesson 4 Webpage planning	
Learning Objective	• Plan a webpage	
Key pedagogy	Get creative	

Activity	Instructions	Guidance
1	• Introduce the project brief (📖 Page 70).	• Set expectations for the amount of detail required, depending on the drawing and writing abilities of your learners.

2	• Explain that there are different types of webpage, using the images (📖 Pages 70 and 71).
	• Demonstrate a variety of webpages.
	• Ask 'What webpages do you enjoy?'
		• You can use webpages of your choice. Include webpages that will be familiar to your class. Here are some suggestions:
		  • National Geographic Kids, 'Animals' tab
		  • Poisson rouge
		  • CBeebies on the BBC website
		  • Unite for literacy
		• Point out webpage features such as headings in big text, images in different shaped boxes, and smaller text. These will be useful later.
		• Encourage learners to think about what they like about the webpages.

Activity	Instructions	Guidance

3	• Remind learners that a website is a collection of webpages. They will be designing one webpage.
	• Remind them that their webpage should be interesting to young children (📖 Page 71).
	• Explain that their webpage could be about a hobby or interest, a place they have visited, a tutorial, or about a topic they have enjoyed at school.
	• Give learners time to come up with a webpage topic, using (📓 Page 56) Task A, 'Choose a topic'.
		• Mention any specific topics that your learners should not choose.
		• Move around the classroom, helping learners to come up with suitable topics. Webpage topics could include:
		  • information about a favourite animal such as a lizard
		  • information about a place they have visited such as a museum or theme park
		  • a webpage with a game such as dressing up a character
		  • a toy shop with descriptions and prices
		  • a recipe for a dessert they enjoy making and eating
		  • a tutorial for drawing a flower
		  • information about a topic they are learning about.

4	• Cover the 'Parts of a webpage' section (📖 Page 71). • Show an example webpage and point out the parts. • Give learners time to complete (📓 Page 56) Task B , 'What is on a webpage?', where they will label a webpage.	• Choose a webpage learners are already familiar with so they can focus on the parts. • You could invite individual learners to point out parts on the webpage.
5	• Give learners time to complete (📓 Page 57) Task C, 'Plan your webpage'. Learners sketch a design for their webpage. • Explain that they are only sketching ideas for their webpage this week. Next week they will work on the final version.	• Encourage learners to focus on the parts of their webpage. They will not have time to add details in this lesson.
6	• Use Discuss 8 (📖 Page 71).	• Show some Workbook examples to the class and ask them to say what they like and what the learner could consider for next lesson. • Make notes on learners' ideas and improvements to use in the next lesson.

Build on this: **Learners could discuss their website sketches in pairs to share ideas.**

Chapter 6:	Lesson 5 Webpage design		
Learning Objective	• Design a webpage		
You will need	• Notes on website ideas from the previous lesson.	**Key pedagogy**	Get creative

Activity	Instructions	Guidance

1	• Remind learners of the project brief and the webpage plans they created in their Workbooks in the previous lesson (📖 Page 72).
	• Use Discuss 9 (📖 Page 72).
		• The discussion question aims to get learners thinking about what a good webpage looks like. You may want to elicit the following features:
		  • colourful
		  • interesting
		  • fun
		  • useful
		  • age-appropriate.

2	• Remind learners of ideas for improvements for their webpages from the previous lesson.	• Use your notes from the previous lesson. • This is also an opportunity to make your expectations clear on how detailed the designs should be and how much real writing learners should include. This will depend on the abilities of your learners and the time available.
3	• Give learners time to complete (📒 Page 58) Task A, 'Age of webpage visitors'. • Use Discuss 10 (📖 Page 72).	• This is an opportunity to remind learners that most webpages are not designed for children. What should they do if they are worried about a webpage? (Tell a grown up.)
4	• Explain that learners will create their final designs in this lesson. • Remind learners to refer to the webpage plans they created in their Workbooks in the previous lesson. • Give learners time to complete (📒 Pages 58 and 59) Task B, 'Design your webpage', where learners sketch and then complete their designs.	• There is a space in the Workbook for sketching and making notes and a full page for creating designs. • There is an additional full page if learners need to start again, or have time to create a second webpage.

Activity	Instructions	Guidance
5	• Use Discuss 11 (📖 Page 72). • Explain that learners will be showcasing their webpages next lesson.	• Remind learners that it's okay to change from their plan if they now have better ideas.

Build on this: Learners could begin to practise showcasing their webpage designs.

Chapter 6:	Lesson 6 Showcase your webpage		
Learning Objective	• Showcase the design of a webpage		
You will need	• Workbooks with completed designs	**Key pedagogy**	Showcase

Activity	Instructions	Guidance
1	• Remind learners what a showcase is and that they will be performing a showcase of their webpage designs in this session. • Run through the tips for showcasing (📖 Page 73).	• Use the illustration in the Student's Book to show how a whole-class showcase might look. • Draw specific attention to how the tips are represented in the illustration, especially the power of using pictures. • If you have time, you could encourage learners to practise with a partner.
2	• Complete the showcase activity (📖 Page 73).	• You could split the class into groups to showcase to each other.
3	• Ask learners to complete (📖 Page 59) Task A, 'Reflection'. They should answer the first two reflection questions by colouring in the number of stars. Guide learners with the task by explaining that colouring five stars is positive and one star is weak. • Congratulate learners for their well thought-out webpages with many key features from webpages on the internet. • Use the Reflect question (📖 Page 74).	

Build on this: Learners could discuss their webpage designs in small groups: what they liked, what they would improve and so on.

Chapter 7 – The power of data
Project: Plan a dream class celebration

Chapter overview

In this chapter, learners will use a search engine to find answers to questions. They will design and complete forms to gather information from many people in their class before sorting and organising the data received. Learners will predict the class results and then analyse the data before visually presenting their findings.

Lesson	Learning Objectives	Summary
Chapter 7: Lesson summary		
1	• Identify ways different devices can be used to answer questions	Learners watch a demonstration of using a search engine and state how to respond to unsafe search results. They take part in a class tally chart to answer a question. Learners complete a multiple-question form.
2	• List different ways devices can sort and organise data	Learners understand that data is used to answer questions by exploring a tally chart. They complete activities to answer questions using sorted, then sorted and organised data. Learners discuss their experiences using different options of displayed data before practising dragging characters in Scratch to sort and organise them.
3	• Design a form to collect categorical data	Learners think about celebrations and draw a picture of how they would like to celebrate. They use input from class discussions to work together and agree on three class questions with options that will be used to plan their celebration.
4	• Collect categorical data using a form	Learners are introduced to an online form containing their questions and observe a demonstration of how to complete their form. They complete the form themselves before using information they have to predict the class results.
5	• Analyse collected categorical data in a data table	Learners practise sorting data in tables to work out the most popular choices. They watch a demonstration of sorting

		class celebration data on a computer before working out which answers were the most popular. They compare the answers with their predictions from the previous lesson.
6	• Present analysis of categorical data to a known audience	Learners draw a picture to visualise the class answers. They showcase their new picture and their individual plan picture from Lesson 3 to a partner and discuss the differences. They reflect on their new data skills and optionally wrap up the Stage 1 Computing syllabus by holding the planned class celebration.

End of chapter project	Plan a dream class celebration
Example ideas that learners could design:	  

Project: Plan a dream class celebration

Name	

	Working towards (1)	Meets expected (2)	Exceeding expected (3)	Score
Sketches	• Online form with answers not sent	• Opened, answered, and sent an online form	• Opened, answered, and sent an online form. Labelled a screenshot identifying key elements	
Final design	• Partially identified the most popular answers	• Identified the most popular answer to each question	• Identified the most popular answer to each question. Discussed the predictions and results.	
Everyday task	• The most popular answers were not clear from the picture	• The data results were shown in the picture	• The data results were shown in the picture. The picture was used as a prop in the showcase.	

Teacher feedback	
Learner response	

Chapter 7:	Lesson 1 Answering questions		
Learning Objective	• Identify ways different devices can be used to answer questions		
New key terms	**search engine** – app that can be used to find information from the internet **form** – document that helps you collect answers to more than one question		
You will need	• A computer to demonstrate a search engine	**Key pedagogy**	Develop practical skills

Activity	Instructions	Guidance
1	• Introduce the chapter (📖 Page 75). • Explain that people ask questions to find out information (📖 Page 76). • Use Discuss 1 (📖 Page 76).	• You could give examples of questions or ask the class to take turns asking questions aloud. • During the discussion you could make a list of the answers that are given (some will be talked about later in the lesson).
2	• Introduce search engines and talk through the search engine cartoon (📖 Page 76). • Demonstrate using a search engine • Use Discuss 2 (📖 Page 76).	• When talking through the cartoon, if hide and seek is not a game familiar to learners, you could mention a game they are familiar with. • When demonstrating using a search engine, make sure you have turned on any safe search features if these are not already filtered out by the school. • When answering the discussion question you could prompt learners to think about what they already know about the internet. You are looking for answers such as: it can search a lot of information; it is connected to websites all over the world; it can search for information quickly.

Activity	Instructions	Guidance
3	• Give learners time to complete (📖🖊 Page 61) Task A, 'Search safely''. • Reinforce the answer 'Tell a grown up'. • Highlight the stay safe message that some search engines have a 'Safe Search' setting.	• Explain how this should work in lesson time. For example, they should tell you if they see something that makes them worried, scared or sad. • If the school has set safe searching on learners' computers, you could tell them this. Explain that it will automatically block some worrying search results and images.
4	• Explain that asking people questions is a good way to find answers (📖 Page 77). • Write a question with a five-option tally chart on the board at the front of the class. For example: 'What is your favourite animal? Lion, Zebra, Snake, Whale or Frog.' • Ask the class to put up their hands if their answer is 'Lion', then tally the number of learners on the board. Repeat for each option. • Count the tally marks to see which is the most popular answer.	• Instead of asking the class to put up their hands, you could ask learners to come to the board and put a tally mark next to their answer. • Choose a question with answer options that are relevant and interesting to your learners.
5	• Explain that sometimes you want to ask someone more than one question and that a form is a good way to do this. Use the image (📖 Page 77) in your explanation. • Give learners time to complete a form themselves, in (📖🖊 Page 62) Task B, 'Fill in the form'. • Use Discuss 3 (📖 Page 77).	• Ask learners to share their Workbook form answers with someone else or to discuss in small groups. • For the discussion question, make connections to any recent examples of forms that have been used in school such as selecting food from a menu.
6	• Give learners time to complete (📖🖊 Page 62) Task C, 'Reflect'.	• Discuss answers as a class and celebrate today's learning.

Build on this: You could give learners a simple question and ask them to use a search engine to practise their typing and use a search engine themselves.

Chapter 7:	Lesson 2 Sort and organise data		
Learning Objective	• List different ways devices can sort and organise data		
New key terms	**data** – information used to answer questions		
You will need	• Scratch project: (Website C7L2R1)	**Key pedagogy**	Develop practical skills

Activity	Instructions	Guidance
1	• Introduce the definition of data (📖 Page 78). • Use Discuss 4 (📖 Page 78) which is related to the cartoon. • Confirm that the data is used to answer the question.	• Remind learners that they saw this tally chart cartoon in lesson one. • Encourage the answer that 'mouse' is the most popular because it has more marks (4) than the others.
2	• Explain 'sorting data' using the description and images (📖 Page 79). • Give learners time to complete (📖 Page 63) Task A, 'Count the tigers', where learners count data in pictures. • Use Discuss 5 (📖 Page 79).	• The picture in the Student's Book is sorted by both shape and colour on this occasion. • The Workbook activity could be run as a timed activity, with learners putting up their hands when they have the answer. • The discussion (and doing the Workbook activity as a timed activity) should highlight that it is quicker and easier to answer questions when the data is sorted.
3	• Explain 'sorting and ordering data' using the description and images (📖 Page 79). • Remind learners that this is not the first time that order has been important, linking back to their learning about algorithms in Chapter 3. • Give learners time to complete (📖 Page 64) Task B, 'Count the insects', where learners count data in pictures. • Use Discuss 6 (📖 Page 79).	• This Workbook activity can be completed as timed exercise again. • In addition to the speed of answering questions, you will probably see accuracy is improved when data is sorted and organised. If so, draw this out in the discussion. • The discussion should highlight that the bottom picture was answered the quickest and with the most accuracy.

| 4 | • Ask learners to open the Scratch project on their computers (Website C7L2R1) and drag the space pictures to sort and order them. | • Running the project full screen makes it easier to drag the characters.
• Learners can reset by clicking on the green flag. |

Build on this: You could lead learners through creating a class tally chart that they can recreate, sort and order on paper.

Chapter 7:	Lesson 3 Plan a celebration
Learning Objective	• Design a form to collect categorical data
Key pedagogy	Get creative

Activity	Instructions	Guidance
1	• Introduce the project brief for this chapter with reference to the images (📖 Page 80). • Use Discuss 7 (📖 Page 80).	• This project could be run purely as a planning exercise or you could actually hold a class celebration during Lesson 6 to celebrate all that learners have achieved during their Stage 1 Computing lessons. • During the discussion, share insight from class celebrations you have run in the past or from how things are celebrated locally.
2	• Give learners time to complete (📖 Page 65) Task A, 'My class celebration', where they draw pictures of how they would like to celebrate. • Use Discuss 8 (📖 Page 80). • Make a note of the answers and group them into themes, explaining to the class how you are grouping their ideas.	• Encourage learners to think about things like food, drink, music and games. • If you are hosting a physical party, you should mention any other choices that learners could make. • If it is an end of term celebration, you might also want them to consider whether parents or other adults from the school staff community would be there.

Activity	Instructions	Guidance
3	• Illustrate that everyone will input into the celebration and that multiple questions will be needed to create a plan (📖 Page 81). • Use Discuss 9 (📖 Page 81). • Use your notes on how learners would like to celebrate and the themes you found to help learners create three questions as a class. Learners should complete (📓 Page 66) Task B, 'Our class form' during this activity, writing down the final questions. • Read through the three agreed questions and tell learners that they will be answering them in the next lesson.	• The questions must allow learners to collect categorical data – data that can be presented in data tables such as tally charts. You could agree on answer choices as you write the questions. • Help the class by sharing some of the themes you noticed from their drawings such as music, food, drink, games or people they would invite. • You could write the short questions on the board as you agree them. This would help learners copy them into their books.

Build on this: Learners could practise their typing by typing the three questions into a word processor.

Chapter 7:	Lesson 4 Collect your data		
Learning Objective	• Collect categorical data using a form		
New key terms	**online form** – webpage with questions for people to answer		
You will need	• A prepared online form using the agreed questions from the previous lesson. There are different solutions for online forms, for example Google Forms.	**Key pedagogy**	Collaboration

Activity	Instructions	Guidance
1	• Introduce online forms using the explanation (📖 Page 82). Tell the class that they will be using an online form to plan their class celebration.	• If it isn't possible to use an online form, you could type the questions and answers in a form layout and print a copy for each learner before the lesson. Learners could complete the form by filling in the printout but you will need to enter their answers into a spreadsheet before the next lesson.

Activity	Instructions	Guidance
2	• Remind learners of the questions they agreed on in the previous lesson. • Show learners the prepared form with their questions. Point out the title, questions, answer types (for example, radio buttons) and the submit button.	• You could direct learners back to their Workbooks to see the questions or show them on a board at the front of class.
3	• Demonstrate completing the form and then ask learners to complete the form on their computers (📖 Page 83). • Learners should complete (📖✏ Page 67) Task A, 'Online form checklist'. They tick off the questions as they complete the form.	• Remind learners to submit their answers when they have completed the form. You could set up a response page for your form with a message to learners so you know when they have submitted it. Check that you receive answers from everyone.

4	• Remind learners what they already know about predicting (📖 Page 83), linking back to Bee-Bot predictions in Chapter 3.
	• Use Discuss 10 (📖 Page 83).
	• This should help learners understand what information will help them predict class results.
	• Ask learners to complete (📖✏ Page 68) Task B, 'My prediction' where they write down their predictions.
	• Use Discuss 11 (📖 Page 83). Tell learners they will have to wait until the next lesson to find out the actual answers.
		• Discussion answers for question 10 could be that learners:
		  • know a bit about what their classmates like and dislike
		  • have discussed their dream party pictures together as a class
		  • have seen/heard reactions to certain answers during class discussion or when completing the form.

Build on this: You could give learners a screenshot of your form and ask them to circle or label key elements such as the submit button.

Chapter 7:	Lesson 5 Use your data		
Learning Objective	• Analyse collected categorical data in a data table		
You will need	• The results from the class form data entry • A prepared spreadsheet with a separate data table for each question	**Key pedagogy**	Develop practical skills

Activity	Instructions	Guidance
1	• Show the example data tables (📖 Page 84). • Use Discuss 12 (📖 Page 84). • Give learners time to complete (📖 Pages 69 and 70) Task A, 'Sort the tables'.	• Learners have seen several examples of data in tables throughout this chapter. They have also looked at a tallied data table and answered questions in an earlier discussion. • They may have used data tables in maths, science or other subjects. • If you have examples on the wall or around the school of data presented in tables, you could point those out.
2	• Pull up the celebration data from the online form on a screen that all learners can see. The data will be in a spreadsheet. • Highlight a row and tell learners that this is one learner's answers to the questions. • Highlight the Question 1 column and tell learners that these are all the answers to question 1.	• If you are using something like Google Forms, open a linked response spreadsheet. This will show each learner entry as a row and the three questions as columns.
3	• Sort the answers in the question 1 column to make them easier to count by right-clicking the column header. • Ask learners to count the number of occurrences of the first answer and work your way down the list. • Ask learners which answer was the most popular for question 1, then tell them to write the number in (📖 Page 70) Task B, 'Popular choices'. • Repeat these steps for the other two questions.	• You could create a summary data table for each question and enter the number of times each answer was given as you work together through the counting. • You could do this on a whiteboard or in the spreadsheet.

Activity	Instructions	Guidance
4	• Use Discuss 13 ([📖] Page 84). • Ask learners to look back at their prediction in the their Workbooks ([📖] Page 70). • Use Discuss 14 ([📖] Page 84).	• If learners have recorded different popular answers, it could be because they had to count and retain the information. You could mention that as well as sorting data, computers can also do the counting. They will learn about that in a later Stage.

Build on this: Learners could discuss the results in pairs. They could talk about why they made their predictions and whether there were any surprises in the data.

Chapter 7:	Lesson 6 Showcase your data		
Learning Objective	• Present analysis of categorical data to a known audience		
You will need	• Your class celebration items if you are holding an actual celebration	**Key pedagogy**	Get creative

Activity	Instructions	Guidance
1	• Explain that pictures are a powerful way to show data. Ask learners if they can spot the food, drink and entertainment answers in each of the three images ([📖] Page 85). • Give learners time to complete ([📖] Page 71) Task A, 'Our class celebration', where they draw a picture of how the class chose to celebrate.	• If you are not holding an actual class celebration, you could photocopy these images and ask learners to circle the chosen food, drink and entertainment in each picture
2	• Run the showcase session, with learners sharing their pictures from this lesson and their pictures from Lesson 3 ([📖] Page 85). • Ask learners to discuss the differences between the initial picture and today's picture.	• If learners are having a class celebration, this showcase can be either a quick discussion with a partner or you can run it a few times with learners moving to different partners to get used to describing their pictures and highlighting differences.

Activity	Instructions	Guidance
3	• Give learners time to complete (📖 Page 72) Task B, 'Reflection', where they reflect on the chapter. They should answer the first two reflection questions by colouring in the number of stars. Guide learners with the task by explaining that colouring five stars is positive and one star is weak. • Use the Reflect question' (📖 Page 86) • End with a celebration of all they have learned in this chapter, including the actual class celebration if you are holding one!	• Remind learners that creating a class celebration together makes a celebration that everyone will enjoy.

Build on this: You could hold a discussion about Computing in Stage 1 to celebrate all learners have achieved across the seven chapters.

Layered scene worksheet

Layer 1

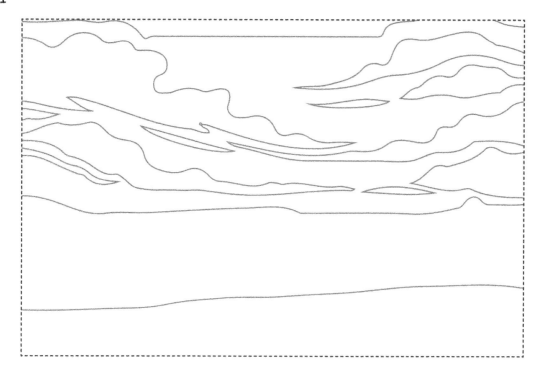

Layer 2

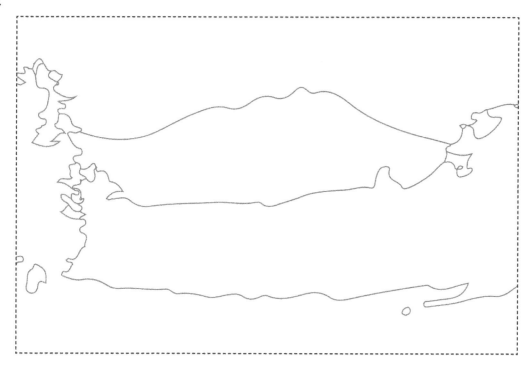

Layered scene worksheet

Layer 3

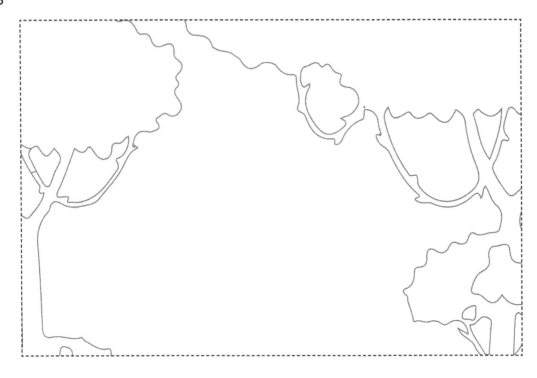

Layer 4

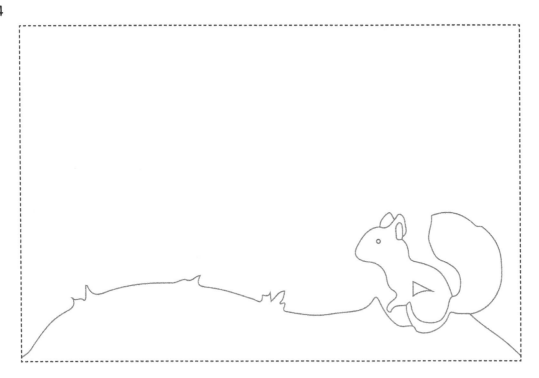

Chapter 1: Our digital world

Chapter 1.1: Computers around you

Task A: Which is not a computer?

1. Hardback book
2. School bag, building blocks

Chapter 2: Content creation

Chapter 2.3: Type your words

Task A: Find the capital

1. A L K P N J H U Q B

Chapter 2.4 Select foods in Scratch

Task A Scratch quiz

1. Stage
2. Yes
3. 6

Chapter 3: Create with code 1

Chapter 3.2: Bee-Bot paths

Task A: Follow a path

1 & 2.

Chapter 3.3: Predict and run

Task A: Label the buttons

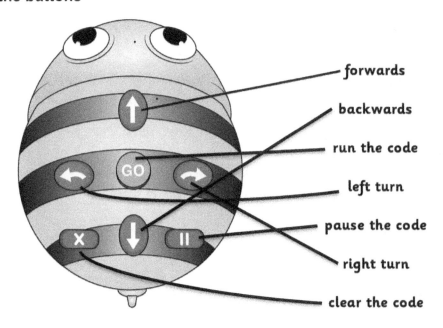

Chapter 4: How computers work

Chapter 4.1: Parts of a computer

Task A: Find the inputs

1. Mouse, touchscreen, keyboard.

Task B: Find the outputs

1. Touchscreen, speakers, printer.

Chapter 4.2: Inputs and outputs in an app

Task A. Investigate a Scratch app

1. a
2. a
3. b
4. b
5. b
6. a

Chapter 4.3: Sound input and output

Task B: Match the pictures

1.

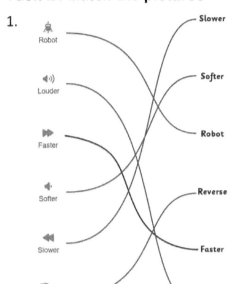

Chapter 4.5: Record sounds for your app

Task B: Where should you click?

1. c

Chapter 5: Create with code 2

Chapter 5.1: Stacking tower

Task B: The correct order

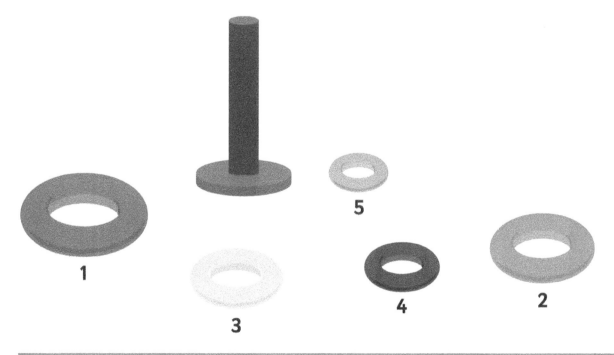

Chapter 5.2: Debugging

Task A: Find the error

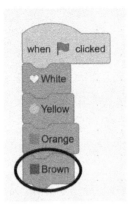

Note that learners may only circle the 'White' block, which is still acceptable at this stage. Technically, they are all in the wrong order.

Task B: Fix the error

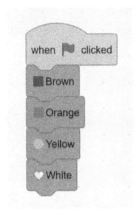

Chapter 5.3: Layered scene

Task A: Order the layers

1. 4
    3
    2
    1

Chapter 6: Connect the world

Chapter 6.1: Wired and wireless connections

Task A: Connect the computer systems

1

A

B

C

Task B: Find the wireless connections

1. a and b should be circled.

Chapter 6.2: Networks and the internet

Task A: Connect to the printer

1. Any combination of wires that connects all computers together.

Task B: Send a message

1. The following scenarios would work:

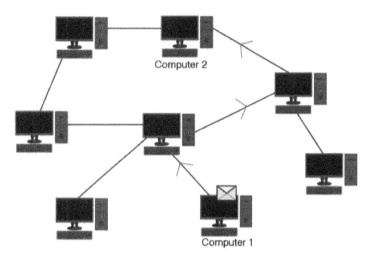

Task C: Connecting to the internet

1. Yes. A tablet computer can connect to the internet with a wireless connection.
2. Yes. A laptop can connect to the internet with a wired or wireless connection.
3. Yes. A smartphone can connect to the internet with a wireless connection.
4. No. There are times when the internet is not available

Chapter 6.3: Web pages and the World Wide Web

Task A: Fill in the letters

1. The World Wide Web is all of the web pages on the internet.
2. A website is a collection of web pages.
3. A webpage is a document that your computer gets from the internet.

Task B: Staying safe

1a. Ask a grown-up if you want to use a computer.

1b. Tell a grown-up if you see something on the computer that worries you.

Chapter 6.4: Web page planning

Task B: What is on a web page?

1.

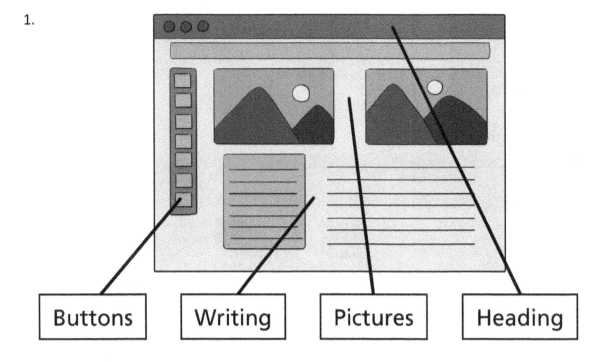

| Buttons | Writing | Pictures | Heading |

Chapter 7: The power of data

Chapter 7.1: Answer questions

Task A: Search safely

1. c

Task C. Reflect

1. B
2. A
3. A

Chapter 7.2: Sort and organise data

Task A: Count the tigers

1. Five
2. Five

Task B: Count the insects

1. Six
2. Ants
3. Four
4. Bees
5. Four
6. Bees

Chapter 7.5: Use your data

Task A: Sort the tables

1a. Art
1b. Sports
1c. Reading
2a. Blue
2b. Pink
2c. Red
3a. Apple
3b. Melon
3c. Grapes

Websites

Introduction

Reference	Website URL
IntR1	https://www.ijcses.org/index.php/ijcses/article/view/15
IntR2	https://link.springer.com/article/10.1007/s10798-021-09692-4
IntR3	https://static.teachcomputing.org/GBIC-Evaluation-Report-Relevance.pdf?ref=blog.teachcomputing.org&_ga=2.107553479.476986320.1697481282-1576158333.1697481282&_gac=1.128134910.1697481282.CjwKCAjwvrOpBhBdEiwAR58-3OfKz8kY2yaeSXvgqUBZEl1hUVK8D2AgJRenXD4M3pmNRzU0PWZGARoC42oQAvD_BwE
IntR4	https://dl.acm.org/doi/10.1145/3373165.3373187
IntR5	https://scholar.google.co.uk/scholar?q=10.1186/s40594-023-00434-7&hl=en&as_sdt=0&as_vis=1&oi=scholart
IntR6	https://ieeexplore.ieee.org/document/9062372
IntR7	https://www.tandfonline.com/doi/full/10.1080/08993408.2011.579805
IntR8	https://scratch.mit.edu/
IntR9	https://www.google.co.uk/forms/about/
IntR10	https://www.google.co.uk/docs/about/

Chapter 2

Reference	Website URL
C2L4R1	https://scratch.mit.edu/projects/892156612/
C2L1R2	https://scratch.mit.edu/

Chapter 4

Reference	Website URL
C4L2R1	https://scratch.mit.edu/projects/910305481/
C4L3R1	https://scratch.mit.edu/projects/892225655/editor/
C4L4R1	https://scratch.mit.edu/projects/912344859/
C4L2R2	https://scratch.mit.edu/projects/912252160/

Chapter 5

Reference	Website URL
C5L1R1	https://scratch.mit.edu/projects/892231035
C5L2R1	https://scratch.mit.edu/projects/1012222705
C5L2R2	https://scratch.mit.edu/projects/1012255566
C5L4R1	https://scratch.mit.edu/projects/913625668
C5L5R1	https://scratch.mit.edu/projects/917569538

Chapter 7

Reference	Website URL
C7L2R1	https://scratch.mit.edu/projects/917340401/fullscreen/